WHO OWI

WHO OWNS ENGLISH?

EDITED BY
**Mike Hayhoe and
Stephen Parker**

Open University Press
Buckingham • *Philadelphia*

Open University Press
Celtic Court
22 Ballmoor
Buckingham
MK18 1XW

and
1900 Frost Road, Suite 101
Bristol, PA 19007, USA

First Published 1994

A catalogue record of this book is available from the British Library

ISBN 0 335 19266 1 (pbk)

Library of Congress Cataloging-in-Publication Data
Who owns English? / edited by Mike Hayhoe and Stephen Parker.
    p. cm. — (English, language, and education series)
   'Papers . . . first presented in March 1993 at the Fifth
International Convention on Language and Education, at the
University of East Anglia'—Pref.
  Includes bibliographical references and index.
  ISBN 0–335–19266–1 (pbk.)
  1. English philology—Study and teaching—Congresses. 2. English
language—Standardization—Congresses. 3. English language—
Variation—Congresses. I. Hayhoe, Mike. II. Parker, Stephen,
1942– . III. International Convention on Language and Education
(5th : 1993 : University of East Anglia) IV. Series.
PE65.W48 1994
420—dc20   93–42511
                                                 CIP

Typeset by Graphicraft Typesetters Ltd., Hong Kong
Printed in Great Britain by St Edmundsbury Press Ltd., Bury St Edmunds, Suffolk

To our present and former colleagues in teacher education – teachers and lecturers alike – whose service has illuminated and inspired the teaching of English.

Contents

List of contributors

Evelyn Arizpe, Doctoral student, Department of Education, University of Cambridge

Suzanne Barton Belote, Hendricks Day School, Jacksonville, Florida, Masters Degree student, University of North Florida

Beverley Bryan, Faculty of Education, The University of the West Indies, Jamaica

Ronald Carter, Professor of Modern English Language, University of Nottingham

David Crystal, Honorary Professor of Linguistics, University College, Bangor

Daniel R. Davis, Assistant Lecturer, Department of English, The University of Hong Kong

P. V. Dhamija, Reader, Department of Phonetics and Spoken English, Central Institute of English and Foreign Languages, Hyderabad

Sean Farren, Senior Lecturer, Faculty of Education, University of Ulster at Coleraine, Northern Ireland

Peter Griffith, Staff Tutor in Education, The Open University

Mary Loftin Grimes, Associate Professor, University of North Florida

Sharon Hamilton, Associate Professor, Department of English, Indiana University, Indianapolis, USA

Bernard Harrison, Reader, Division of Education, University of Sheffield

Dianne Sirna Mancus, Professor of Education, Rice University, Houston, Texas, USA

Aya Marbach, Lecturer, Oranim Teacher Education College and teacher, Hareali High School, Haifa, Israel

John Marenbon, Fellow, Trinity College, Cambridge

Acknowledgements

We are grateful to the following for permission to reproduce material:

- The author and Universal Press Syndicate for an extract from one of Bill Watterson's *Calvin and Hobbes* cartoon strips.
- The author and Faber & Faber for Seamus Heaney's poem *The Other Side*.
- The Blackstaff Press for John Hewitt's poem *Once Alien Here*.

Preface

The chapters of this book were first presented in March 1993 as papers at the Fifth International Convention on Language and Education, at the University of East Anglia. The convention's members came from over twenty countries across the globe, their varied topics and views creating a rich event – but the constant centre of debate was the nature of English and the rights and responsibilities of those who use it. These chapters show the seriousness of discussion that took place and in particular the intensity of views about the roles of governments and peoples in laying claims to its ownership.

At a time of increasing insecurity and a declining sense of national identity, the popular demand for scapegoats and solutions has been met in England and Wales by the increasing intervention of the state and its setting up a centralized curriculum with powerful accountability methods. Their vision, it seems to many critics, has been to raise (or restore) standards in the nation's language, heritage and ethics by means of centralizing, legislative prescription: a movement towards standards through standardization, including the enforcement of Standard English.

The seductive solution of attempting to guarantee results through the imposition of uniformity is debated in several chapters, often with reference to parallel patterns of official dissatisfaction and enforced change in other countries, such as Mexico, Israel and the United States of America. But other chapters present a different attitude towards English, seeing popular language change and the existence of divergence not as evidence of decline or as a cause for concern but as a cause for excitement and optimism. For these authors, language shift is evidence of people taking ownership of English and adjusting it to the needs of their cultures and their times, enabling it to take a variety of forms across the world.

These two attitudes – of governmental conservatism and popular optimism – weave their way throughout this book, raising issues for those of us who work in the classroom, the place where we and our students meet and must needs cope with both perspectives. This volume gives no easy answers but its many questions display the liveliness of the current debate and demonstrate the importance of our being informed members of it, as we seek to find positive ways of ensuring that our students are aware of their rights – and their responsibilities – in owning their English.

Mike Hayhoe and Stephen Parker

General editor's introduction

The papers that comprise this volume are among those given at the latest of the biennial conferences on the teaching and learning of English held at the University of East Anglia. The conference itself included the presentation of many other papers of considerable importance, of which only a relatively small selection are able to be included here. That the meeting attracted such great international interest was undoubtedly due to the combination of the issues of language and politics implicit in its title.

For me, such a title inevitably recalls the work of George Orwell and in my own paper, co-presented at the conference with my colleague, Witold Tulasiewicz, on 'The Rhetoric of Teacher Education', not included here, we began by quoting his seminal *Horizon* (April, 1946) essay, 'Politics and the English Language.'

It is a matter of never-ending surprise (and some concern) to note how contemporary a feel his words have even after nearly 50 years. In this essay Orwell writes:

> In our time it is broadly true that political writing is bad writing . . . The political dialects to be found in pamphlets, leading articles, manifestos, White Papers and the speeches of Under-Secretaries do, of course, vary from party to party, but they are all alike in that one almost never finds in them a fresh, vivid, home-made turn of speech . . . In our time, political speech and writing are largely the defence of the indefensible. If thought corrupts language, language can also corrupt thought . . .

Many of the papers presented at the meeting explored language in such contexts, especially the way, in much contemporary political discourse, one discerns an appeal to the 'common-sense' of the 'ordinary person'; a kind of populism that distrusts any kind of expertise. In England and Wales, in the wake of the introduction of the National Curriculum, this has been more apparent in the case of English than any other subject, and it is the source of the violent political controversy that has bedevilled much of the discussion of the English National Curriculum Orders since their inception. Inevitably this was the topic of several of the contributions to the conference and those represented here indicate the range of argument that was advanced on all sides of the political debate. But the debate ranged much more widely than over matters of domestic politics and policies alone. Many of the concerns explored by overseas speakers mirrored very closely the debate taking place in the United Kingdom. All were considerably aware of the issues of language and identity and, especially, of the issue of ownership of language. The desire to preserve a 'pure' language, the notion that this is to be enshrined in a particular form, such as that implicit in the notion of a 'Standard English', was a theme addressed by many speakers. We have seen, often all too tragically in recent years, the folly of the over-close identification of language with narrow nationalist aspirations and, in many ways, the identification of a national 'standard' form of the language (often in association with the notion of a nationalist canon of literature) in an attempt by some politicians to unite a country that some see as losing its identity in a multi-cultural, multi-faith, and multi-lingual society.

These issues never remain static, however. One of my present research students, coming from Malaysia, has written a paper for me about how her own country tried through its educational system to impose a national identity by insisting on the use of the Malaysian language in the curriculum, only to find later that the reintroduction of the medium of English in the schools became an economic and political necessity. Another such student, Evelyn Arizpe, addresses some of the same issues in a Mexican context in her contribution to this volume.

The real question which the conference as a whole seemed to me to be addressing, as the papers presented began to come together into a remarkable unity of concern, was that of the ownership of English together with the related questions of where contemporary English comes from and where it is going to. As English becomes ever more a language of international importance it is clear that its ownership can no longer be restricted to the inhabitants of the British Isles. It may well be, as one of the presenters suggested, that we shall see an increased divergence in the Englishes spoken worldwide and the 'English' of England will become an increasingly minor variety of 'world English'. Certainly the English that is becoming rapidly the language used in conferences within the European Union is becoming a new variety of the language with a number of idiolects of its own.

This makes it even more important than ever in the teaching of English in all English-speaking countries that we should use a wide variety of texts drawn from as many traditions and cultures as possible. It is no longer possible, if it ever was, to think in terms of a 'pure well of English, undefiled'. Those who seek, in the cause of a mistaken nostalgia, to impose this upon the schools do a serious disservice to the language they seek to perpetuate. The 'genius of the language' so far as English is concerned is that it has always been willing and eager to accommodate change and this is a main source of its strength as a world language today. The quality of the presentations at the University of East Anglia made this abundantly clear and I am glad that we have been able to give so truthful a representation of the excitement of the convention in the papers it has been possible to collect together in this volume.

Anthony Adams

1 English, the government and the curriculum

JOHN MARENBON

I

In recent years, the teaching of English at school has become an area of political as well as intellectual controversy. Traditionalists, who believe in old-fashioned methods of teaching reading and writing, and in a literary canon, are ranged against progressives. Those who want to emphasize what they regard as the basics are set against those who insist on a broader conception of the subject. Is there any way to resolve, if not these differences, then at least the practical difficulties and antagonisms they create? I shall suggest that there is a way, but that it can be found only by beginning not from problems about English, but from a more general question. What, we should begin asking, is the basis of government's right to regulate the curriculum?

Two different sorts of answer to this question are implied by the various utterances of politicians: one is linked to notions of accountability, the other to the legal obligation of parents to educate their children. Both are reflected in different ways by the legislation for the National Curriculum, which is compulsory only for those at publicly-funded schools, and which applies only to the years of compulsory schooling.

The argument for accountability runs like this: *Premise One*: as the steward of taxpayers' money, the government is responsible for seeing that it is well spent. *Premise Two*: a great deal of taxpayers' money is spent on schooling. *Conclusion*: the government is therefore responsible for the content of schooling. The two premises given here are indeed irrefragable. But the conclusion does not follow from them. That this is so can easily be seen from parallel but simpler cases. If I pay a lawyer or a doctor for his professional services, he is without doubt directly accountable to me. But this does not mean that I expect to be able to dictate the legal arguments which the one will use, or the diagnosis which the other will provide. Unless I can rely on their professional judgement, it is in vain that I look to them for assistance. There is a closer parallel. Many parents do pay schools directly to educate their children. They do not expect, however, to decide what the schools teach them. A school's particular curriculum may be one of the reasons why one set of parents chooses this private school rather than that one, but this suggests a quite different way of understanding accountability than that which would make it lead to regulation – a way whereby accountability is seen to be ensured by the providing of choice. There is an important corollary which emerges from the failure of the argument from accountability. If financial accountability does not provide grounds for regulating the school curriculum, it follows that there is no good reason for excluding fee-paying schools from whatever curricular arrangements are imposed on maintained ones. This is not a reason for requiring private schools to follow the National Curriculum – at least not in anything like its present form. Rather, it suggests that the feeling which made ministers hold back from imposing these controls on independent schools should also have held them back from applying such controls to any school at all.

It is, then, to the legal obligation on all parents to ensure that their children receive full-time education between the ages of 5 and 16 that we need to look in order to find a basis for governmental rights to control over the curriculum. Receiving a full-time education means more than spending a certain number of hours in a building called a school. And there are certain curricular arrangements which, nearly everyone would agree, would not properly constitute a full-time education. For example, almost no one would consider that a normal child had received a proper full-time education if at some time he had not been taught some mathematics or, by contrast, if mathematics were all that he was ever taught. Still, until very recently, governments have been satisfied that they were ensuring that parents met their legal obligations without having any form of National Curriculum. It was enough to exercise some control over schools and their staffing and then to leave it to headteachers and teachers to decide on what was taught. There are two good reasons why such a relaxed arrangement would need to be ended. First, it might become clear that at least some substantial minority of teachers and schools were not providing important elements which would generally be considered to be part of a compulsory full-time education. Second, it might become evident that intermediary bodies between central government and individual schools, such as local authorities and inspectorates, or those responsible for teacher training , or even the central school inspectorate (HMI), were imposing very tight constraints on what was taught, limiting the freedom of individual schools and teachers. If this were the case, a limited National Curriculum could liberate schools by making it absolutely clear what teaching was requisite in all cases and how much room there was outside that for individual choices. Probably both these conditions – certainly the second – were fulfilled in the decade or so before 1987, when the government instituted its plans for a national curriculum. The government did not, then, lack grounds for imposing some sort of curriculum. But what was justifiable was a very limited curriculum – one which ensured that no child's compulsory education was so deficient or eccentric that it was an education in name only.

This becomes even clearer if we ask what is the basis for making full-time schooling from 5 to 16 itself a legal obligation. The state is right to interfere with the freedom of parents in this way, because it has a duty, not only to them as citizens, but to the citizens which their children will become. But if the children are denied an education, this is not something that they can make up, or at least make up fully, when they, as adults, can decide for themselves. There are, indeed, many important skills and areas of knowledge, necessary for life, which are learned at home, from parents, siblings, friends, in the early years of life and in the course of everyday experience throughout life. But there are other skills and areas of knowledge, also necessary for anyone who is to live a normal life in a modern society, which usually require instruction by teachers with special learning and experience: reading, writing, basic mathematics, basic science. These might, with every justification, be included in a national curriculum. Almost everybody would agree on their necessity; but, equally, on their insufficiency. No education which consisted just of such training would, even in the barest sense, be complete.

Among the most obvious candidates, beyond these, for the constituents of an education are, on the one hand, some higher cognitive capabilities, such as mathematical and scientific reasoning, distinctively literary appreciation, the aesthetic understanding of music and visual arts, and, on the other hand, those areas of knowledge which place a person as heir to the collective past of the society in which he lives: the literary, artistic and philosophical masterpieces of past generations and the history of his country and continent, its turning-points, institutions and ideas.

I would wish to argue the place of all these in any education. But I would not wish a government to prescribe them in a national curriculum, for this reason. If I wish government to prescribe beyond the narrow area of necessary learning about which there is agreement, I must be willing to accept what is prescribed, whether it is what I would wish or not. I know that many people would have quite different candidates from mine for inclusion as constituents of the curriculum. Some might think far more in terms of the child's personal development, others in terms of practical skills for the world of work. They would all have their arguments and, however strong I think mine are, I could not be sure that they would prevail. Indeed, I could be fairly sure that none of the arguments would be entirely accepted or rejected and that government, weak on logic but strong on compromise, would fill the rest of the curriculum with a selection of what we all wanted, delighted that it had steered a middle course and unconcerned that the mish-mash it had sanctioned would not provide a good education for anyone. And even if one government promised me that it would prescribe what I wanted, I would resist the temptation to turn my considered preferences into law, mindful of the ease with which the same provisions could be used to make compulsory what I thought unnecessary or harmful.

Prescription, then, should be limited to the very core of knowledge and skills, about the necessity of which there really is general agreement, and any national curriculum should have two parts: clear, direct prescription in these fields; and an equally clear directive to the effect that this area of prescription does not constitute an education. Education is much more, but it is not for government to decide what it should be.

II

In the light of these principles, what should be the main features of a national curriculum in English? Despite the many different views which there are about English teaching, there is very widespread agreement that schools should teach their pupils to read fluently and accurately, and to write Standard English correctly, using a reasonably wide vocabulary. Possibly in the 1960s or early 1970s there were some extremists who placed little or no premium on teaching pupils to write Standard English, but even then they were, I believe, few and far between, and today I do not imagine that there are any. Here, then, is an important area of agreement in a subject where controversies abound – so long, of course, as we can resist trying to lay down which methods must be used to achieve these common purposes. No curriculum should do that. But a curriculum might justifiably lay down these aims as being ones to which all English teachers should aspire, as necessary though by no means sufficient conditions for teaching the subject.

Should a national curriculum in English go beyond this fairly well-defined area where there is a good measure of agreement? Two further aspects of English which many would wish to include within any national curriculum are speaking and listening on the one hand, and the literary tradition on the other. Speaking and listening are considered by most English teachers nowadays to be an essential part of the subject, along with reading and writing; and industrialists emphasize the practical value of these skills and their importance to Britain as a competitive, commercial nation. The literary tradition is, by contrast, a notion with which most English teachers (whatever their dedication to teaching literature) are uncomfortable. But many people outside the profession are attached to the notion and consider children have missed an important part of their education if they do not leave school having read some of the acknowledged great English authors.

To anyone of my generation, at school in the 1960s and early 1970s, one of the most surprising features of English teaching at school today is the widespread acceptance of speaking and listening as component parts of the subject, equal in status to reading or writing. Of course, plenty of speaking and listening went on in English lessons when I was at school – plenty went on in any lesson at any time: how else can teaching and learning take place? But we were not encouraged to think of aptitudes in speaking or listening as ones to be separately assessed. Nor were we given classroom tasks designed specifically to develop and test our powers of speaking and listening.

There is, I believe, room to question whether today's approach is beneficial.

Speaking and listening are indeed necessary skills for life. But are they ones which need to be taught specially at school? Are they not skills which are learned at home, in the general course of life and at school in the course of every activity, from a physics lesson to the lunch-break?

But, the argument goes, some children will never be very forthcoming in speech unless they are given special encouragement, since they are shy in character or they come from a family background where speaking is not much encouraged. To which I would reply by asking whether it is for the school to try to change a child's character or, having as it were passed a negative judgement on a particular family background, to try to rescue the child from what the *bien pensants* consider to be its ill effects. And, even supposing that we accepted the need for such teaching in these cases, should what is required to correct an exceptional disadvantage, if we call it that, be instituted as a rule for everyone? We might, moreover, question whether loquacity is such a good thing, and ask whether we are training a generation able and willing to speak but with nothing to say. I remember a picture in the National Gallery, a portrait of a man in thought, which sports the inscription: 'Either be silent, or speak what is better than silence.' How many nowadays pay heed to this injunction?

But what, you ask, will I do to ensure that children learn to speak Standard English? I answer that the notion of spoken Standard English is, to say the least, a dubious one, but, so far as it can made intelligible, there is no good reason at all why children should, as a matter of policy, be taught to speak Standard English at all.

Those who advocate the teaching of spoken Standard English usually present it as an oral equivalent of written Standard English, although they add that certain constructions are permissible in speech which are not in writing and sometimes they even put forward the idea that correct spoken Standard English will contain a number of mistakes, although how they explain this paradox I do not know. Yet spoken English is not, in fact, simply written English spoken. Spoken English is a stream of sounds, an adequate description of which contains many features not found in written English, and some not even captured by a good phonetic transcription. Almost everyone who advocates the teaching of spoken Standard English emphasizes strongly that no particular way of pro-nouncing English should be taught. But what is spoken English stripped of its pronunciation? It may be that what these advocates have in mind is that pupils should learn to speak English in such a way that, if it were transcribed into ordinary written words, it would not contain certain obvious grammatical errors of written Standard English ('We was going', 'I didn't do nothing'). This is a strangely abstract and negative principle on which to base a universal pedagogy! Why, we might also ask, when we are all happy that children should retain a particular accent and intonation peculiar to their region or back-ground, do we not allow them to keep features of grammar and lexis which are equally the reflection of their origins and which belong to the way of speaking evident in their pronunciation? And, while the position of Standard written

English as the language of culture and business, literature and politics need be in no doubt, is there any one variety of spoken English which has such preeminence?

A person's way of speaking – not just accent and tone, but grammar, syntax and choice of words – is intimately connected with his conception of himself, the sort of person he is, what his roots are, who his friends are, what his aspirations are. To adopt, or to acquiesce in growing into, certain manners of speech is a way to express or accept loyalty to a certain group and to distance oneself from other groups. Governments should not, and cannot, break down this function of speech as self-definition. Nor should the classroom be the laboratory in which this experiment is attempted, for fear that tensions and resentments so generated will prevent it from being a place where children come to add wider loyalties to their parochial ones and join, if with a scarce audible whisper, in the conversation of mankind.

None of what I have said means that I would like to see speaking and listening banned as a separate classroom activity, or that all attempts to teach children to speak Standard English, whatever this may mean, should be banned. Indeed, I have some sympathy for the idea that children who speak dialects which are difficult to understand for most people outside their area might be taught a form of speech more readily comprehensible in the country as a whole rather in the way people learn a second language. Different teachers, different schools, different parents all should be allowed to exercise their own choices. But speaking and listening should not form a compulsory part of a national curriculum, nor should the dubious concept of spoken Standard English feature within it.

III

I turn now to the second of these areas which some people, though not everyone, believe should feature in a national curriculum for English: the literary tradition. The idea of a literary tradition is closely linked in people's minds with that of a literary canon. Certainly, the two notions have it in common that they instantly raise the hackles of almost every teacher of English, at school or university. And it is true, too, that someone who, like myself, is happy to talk about the literary tradition will probably also happily refer to a literary canon, or rather canons. Yet, in spite of this, the debate about canonicity, whatever its place in discussions about English at university, is largely irrelevant so far as English teaching at school is concerned. The reason for this is that not even the most rigid canonist could possibly complain that, in their choice of pre-twentieth-century literature to be studied, teachers and exam boards tend to choose uncanonical authors. On the contrary, the complaint must be rather that only the most obvious, most readily accepted as great authors are included. Often, indeed, study of pre-twentieth-century literature is narrowed down to just the one author whom even the anti-canonists accept as canonical: Shakespeare.

As this point itself indicates, the real question about the teaching of literature at schools concerns the extent to which the literary tradition is studied at all. It is a matter of emphasis, since no teacher, I think, would stick entirely to the twentieth century, nor would anyone suggest that modern and indeed contemporary writing did not have a place in the schoolroom. What balance should be struck between the acknowledgedly great authors of previous centuries and second-, third- or fourth-rate writing from our own times? (There are, of course, some acknowledgedly great twentieth-century authors, but most of them are notoriously difficult and can probably only be sampled gingerly, even by the brightest pupils, at least in the years of compulsory schooling).

I believe that a great deal of weight should be given to the great authors of the past. Partly this is a matter of quality. Were 'literature' a straightforwardly descriptive term (even if for human artefacts), like the terms 'prose', 'oil painting' or 'piano concerto', it might be possible to gain an understanding of what it involved from any group of instances of it whatever. But in fact the very notion of literature is itself a complicated construct, rooted in a particular set of traditions and cultures and inseparably linked to the particular works which have been taken pre-eminently to exemplify it. Unless he comes to know some of these great works, a person will remain ignorant of what literature is, as a matter not merely of theoretical but also of practical understanding. He will be cut off for ever from the cognitive values which structure our understanding of literature.

Moreover, even modern literature is part of a literary tradition. Its authors are conscious of the works of the past and their writing is often rich in allusions to them. The understanding of any segment of the literary tradition is incomplete when it is taken in isolation.

The literary tradition is both of the present and yet also of the past. When we read a text as literature, we do not, in the manner of an intellectual historian, use our understanding of its time to make a third-person reconstruction of the text as the intentional artefact which it was designed to be, but rather we read the text directly, regarding it – perhaps quite contrary to its author's intentions – as literature in our post-romantic sense. We accommodate the text to our sense of what it should be and so make it live for us, without its losing altogether its pastness, its rootedness in another time and set of assumptions. Most English teachers these days are commendable in their enthusiasm to introduce their pupils to a variety of cultures by reading texts from the many English-speaking countries around the world. But cultural diversity (and continuity) is chronological as well as geographic. An airliner can transport us effortlessly to the remotest regions of the globe; literature alone can make the past live for us when we make it live in our present.

And literature also gives us a map of our past. The literary tradition shows us how we came to be what we are. It is hard to hear, without a smile, accounts of Hegel reading out his *Phenomenology of Spirit* to the schoolchildren he was supposed to be teaching. It may be a good thing to stretch children to their utmost, but that was going a bit too far! Yet something which children do need, if they are to be properly educated, is, not perhaps Hegel's *Phenomenology* but *a* phenomenology of spirit, a way of grasping how our ways of thought and understanding have developed and come to be what they are, a history of ourselves as human beings and inheritors of a particular cultural and wider human tradition. It is just this grasp which is frequently lacking in otherwise well-educated school-leavers. A study of the literary tradition is one of the best and easiest ways to gain it.

You will object to all of what I am saying that it is far too demanding: perhaps for the brightest pupils from the most cultivated backgrounds at the 'best' schools it makes some sense, but what about the inner city comprehensive? But this objection underestimates the extent to which great literature deals with ideas and emotions which are of interest and importance to all people at any time, and how powerfully it communicates even when its finer nuances are missed. Yes, indeed, great care must be taken to match the text to the pupil. Care in its presentation is needed; patience, effort and imagination: all qualities which the best English teachers have in abundance. We should not allow ourselves to be swayed by the easy philistinism which mocks the idea that ordinary teenagers might read and enjoy Milton and Dr Johnson, as if the latter were too effete and the former too savage for there to be any common meeting ground.

Despite all these reasons for thinking that it is important for schoolchildren to study the literary tradition, and possible for them to do so with understanding and enjoyment, it does not follow that a national curriculum should insist on the study of the great literary classics of the past, nor indeed that it should contain any prescriptions for the reading of literature, beyond the bare requirement that literature should, in some form, be studied. A properly minimal national curriculum need not enter at all into questions about what literature pupils read. But if there is to be a more extensive national curriculum, then the literary tradition should be given an important place in its requirements.

IV

To conclude, the present National Curriculum in English is a good example of what might be called 'liberal collectivism' – liberal both in its openness to progressive ideas and also in the sense of 'liberal' in 'liberal arts' or a 'liberal education': it suggests a wide view of the subject, not quite one I would share but, none the less, a challenging and constructive one. It is collectivist because it imposes this view of the teaching of the subject as a whole on every teacher and every pupil. The revised English curriculum proposed by the National Curriculum Council is – for the converse reasons – an example of 'illiberal collectivism'. What I have tried to advocate in curricular matters, and in the English curriculum in particular, is what might be called a 'conservative pluralism' – pluralism because, in all that goes beyond a small widely agreed core of necessary skills and knowledge, it grants complete freedom to schools, teachers and parents; conservative, because it stems not from any view that one approach is no better than another or that every opinion, every cultural preference must be taken and valued solely on its own terms, but rather from a distrust of governmental attempts to regulate the detail of individuals' lives, and the settled conviction that most great projects for general improvement end in failure and disillusion.

The title of the conference at which this chapter was presented as a paper posed a question: English, whose English? It is not a question to which, collectively, we can give an answer at all. But for each of us, individually, the answer is simple. Whose English? Our English – because in that word 'our' we each express at once our individuality and our belonging to those smaller and larger, particular and more general communities and traditions, from which we have come to be what we are and in which we find ourselves.

2 Standard Englishes in teaching and learning

RONALD CARTER

The victory of one reigning language (dialect) over the others, the supplanting of languages, their enslavement, the process of illuminating them with the True Word, the incorporation of barbarians and lower social strata into a unitary language of culture and truth, the canonisation of ideological systems, philology with its methods of studying and teaching dead languages, languages that were by that very fact 'unities', Indo-European linguistics with its focus of attention, directed away from language plurality to a single proto-language – all this determined the content and power of the category of 'unitary language' in linguistic and stylistic thought.

(Bakhtin, 1981)

Introduction

This chapter pursues two main themes. The first explores the differences and distinctions between spoken and written English, with particular reference to grammar. It will be argued that teachers need to know more about this than about most aspects of language. It is an under-researched area but some recent research findings by linguists will be reported, for such a focus has vital implications for literacy development. Differences between speech and writing are also one of the most stimulating and creative sources, particularly in literary and media texts, for developing a knowledge about language which may feed both directly into pedagogy and into an enhancement of spoken and written language skills. The second theme is more subsidiary but no less important: the need for teachers to understand better some of the discourses surrounding the English language and English language teaching – the need, for example, to know about, understand and contest the variable social discourses which underlie keywords such as *proper, correct, standard, national, grammar, drill* and, most prominently, the key word *English* itself. In fact, it will be argued that these two themes conveniently converge in several current debates concerning the place of English in the National Curriculum. Definitions of spoken and written English are the source of much continuing confusion concerning what is correct and proper English, what is grammar and, above all, what constitutes Standard English.

Grammar and writing

It is frequently the case that literacy debates, particularly as conducted in the national media, take place in the absence of attestable evidence, thus ensuring that rising or declining standards of literacy are simply established by the clearest assertions and by the most forceful anecdotes. However, it is also not unusual for debates internal to the profession to be conducted without detailed scrutiny of language data. It seems appropriate therefore for the discussion in this chapter to be based on data. The first examples here are drawn from language produced by children in material collected in the course of the Language in the National Curriculum Project (LINC) between 1989 and 1992. At this stage it is simplest for them to be classified as examples of 'spoken' grammar:

Examples of 'spoken' grammar

1. *left-displaced subject* (with recapitulatory pronoun)
   The man with the loud voice he said.
   The women they all shouted.
2. *right-displaced subject* (with amplificatory noun-phrase tag)
   It was a really big explosion that one.
   He was an outstanding leader was Robson.
3. *repeated main verb in main clause*
   There's a few problems are likely to crop up.
4. *double relative pronoun*
   There's another person who I don't know what she's responsible for.
5. *'complete' relative clause*
   Which is why we put the Bunsen-burner on a low flame.
6. *Wh-pseudo cleft* (as 'summarizing conjunctions')
   What I would do is people should try a different policy.
7. *double main verb*
   The problem is is I don't how to solve it.
8. *verbless clauses*
   With a very large house in its own grounds.
9. *elliptical phrases*
   Jill likes the rock group, myself the folk.
10. *fronted anticipatory phrase*
    That house in Brentford Street, is that where she lives?

(LINC, 1992)

The following observations can be made:

1. The examples are attested, authentic, 'real'.
2. It is not a comprehensive list by any means but it is representative of aspects of regular English usage. The examples belong more to the spoken language domain than to the domain of written language but are regularly found in pupils' writing.
3. They are all examples of *standard* English. Many of these same grammatical features are used *standardly* by educated users of English and are not uncommonly found in television and radio discussion programmes.
4. They are not described by the standard descriptive grammars of English; indeed, some of the definitions sound more appropriate to ice-skating rather than language study (one can, for example, imagine Torvill and Dean performing a right-displaced subject with amplificatory noun-phrase tag). The reason for this is that all the most authoritative, standard grammars are based on written examples or on examples of very formal contexts of spoken English. There is a neat circularity here. No recognized descriptive terms exist because the forms are not recognized as part of the standard grammar.
5. An example of this situation is Randolph Quirk *et al.*'s *A Comprehensive Grammar of the English Language* (1985). It draws its examples from a very small corpus of $1\frac{1}{2}$ million words. The corpus is mostly written text and what limited spoken data there is is based on conversations between university dons in a University of London common room in the 1960s. It may be doing university dons in the 1960s a disservice, but it would be surprising if the English used in that context was anything other than a quite restricted code. But that quite restricted code is nevertheless used as a basis for definitions of what is standard English grammar.

It is important, however, that we acknowledge some of the reasons for a situation in which our view of grammar is bound up with the written language to the extent that *grammar* may be best defined as grammar of *written* English.

One obvious reason for this phenomenon is that until very recently written language was all that was available for detailed scrutiny. Even now very sophisticated technology is needed to collect spoken data properly. Written language is simply more available and collectable. This is one of the reasons why the history of linguistics has been, until the advent of discourse analysis in the late 1970s and 1980s, the history of the study of written language systems. It is one of the reasons why Dr Johnson did not record certain words in his dictionary of 1765. Johnson pronounced that words such as *sham, snob, bamboozle, flimsy* were ephemeral and would not last beyond a few years. They were merely spoken uses and could not be attested in written sources. They could not therefore have the standardized authority accorded to them by inclusion in a dictionary.

Another reason for this situation (and this reason cannot be easily divorced from the previous one) is that written language has more prestige. It has also been seen as something you have to learn and is indeed a mark of learning to the extent that, for many people, literacy is synonymous with the ability to read and write, while an illiterate is ignorant, lacking in intelligence and even mentally deficient. Many of the most canonical writers in the language such as Dickens, Hardy, Lawrence (and to a lesser extent Elizabeth Gaskell) have not solved the problem of the power of standard orthography for the representation of authentic spoken English. Such characters as are accorded the distinction of speaking real, informal or non-standard spoken English are inevitably therefore represented as uneducated, as unintelligent, or, at best, simply idiosyncratic.

One main danger, therefore, is that spoken English continues to be judged by the codified standards of written English, and that teaching pupils to speak standard English may, in fact, be to teach them to speak in formal written English. A test of spoken English may, therefore, become a test of one's abilities to speak a very restricted code – a formal English used routinely by dons, civil servants and cabinet ministers. It is the language of formal debate which is why a return to tests of the skills of formal debating may be likely. Such a view of spoken English can produce an artificial and unnatural English and can even promote a kind of illiteracy which is as damaging as not being able to write literate English. To have everyone speaking one *code* – a standard written English – generates an illiteracy almost as grave as would be the case if everyone were only able to use a local dialect.

To summarize, it has been argued so far

• that there is a close relationship between standard English and the written language.
• that there are forms of spoken English which are perfectly standard and which are indeed grammatically correct. These forms do not appear in standard grammars, however, and it is easy, therefore, for them to be judged as non-standard and ungrammatical.
• that there are dangers inherent in teaching children to speak formal written English structures or indeed testing them for their ability to speak, in effect, like a book.

It is vital that teachers know more about such questions for they will then be better equipped to help pupils to know more about one of the most central features of language and literacy. It will be argued later that such understandings are best promoted by pedagogic processes which involve regular comparison and contrast of spoken and written texts and not by processes which focus on one to the exclusion of the other.

Language and relativism

There is also a further danger. It is that a proper view of these essential distinctions and differences between spoken and written English should not allow too relativistic a view to prevail. It would be both inaccurate linguistically and disempowering for learners to understand that written and spoken language are *wholly* different and distinct systems.

It has indeed been argued that there are dangers in allowing too writerly a view of language and grammar but this should not obscure the fact that there *is* a *core* of grammatical features which are common and central to both standard spoken and written Englishes.

For example:

- subject/verb agreement and subject/pronoun agreement (e.g. 'the men go that way' rather than 'the men goes that way');
  consistency of tenses across clause and sentence boundaries;
  the avoidance of adjectives in place of adverbs;
  (e.g. not 'he did brilliant' or 'he played exceptional' but rather 'brilliantly', 'exceptionally')
- the avoidance of double or multiple negation except for the expression of tentativeness . . . ('we are not uninterested . . .' which expresses a tentative proposition but not 'We can't do nothing about it').

Split infinitives are also regularly cited in this connection as an example of a grammatical form which should be consistently avoided in all contexts of English usage, spoken and written, even though this particular form is convention bound rather than rule-bound. For some users it is a social convention universally to avoid splitting infinitives but the convention is based on language use in Latin grammar and, as Bernard Shaw pointed out, cannot be a rule codified within English grammar. It is a matter of style and is peripheral to standard grammar in a way that, for example, subject verb agreement is central.

The *core* features are standard in English writing in all but the most informal spoken contexts and it is dishonest and unduly relativistic to pretend otherwise. The criticisms from the extreme right in current English policy-making have some validity here. There is a real danger in the essentially romantic doctrine which accepts as valid the language children produce simply because it is theirs and therefore part of *their* individual, social and cultural identity. There is a further real danger in refusing to accept another criticism from the right that there has been an undue and uncritical emphasis on what children already know and can do and on what they bring to school rather than on what they do not know, cannot do or on what the school can bring to them.

It is, in my view, necessary for teachers of English to accept the challenges to us to review our practices and, if necessary, to modify them. It is not appropriate to dismiss criticism simply because it is right-wing criticism or emerges from a very narrow and unrepresentative pressure group. There is some truth to the charges of a relativistic romanticism and to the charges that teachers are unwilling to tell and teach core facts about the language because such practices appear transmissive and authoritarian or may appear to prioritize teaching over learning. The new version of the National Curriculum English Order (DFE, 1993) may help us to avoid the worst excesses of relativism by stressing the core features which are common to standard spoken *and* written English. And that is good. I think we must also accept that, by being weighted towards a written model of the language, it may insufficiently reflect the continua which exist between the written and the spoken. That is less good.

Our teaching will therefore have to maximize the situation to ensure that pupils develop a rich repertoire of spoken and written functions, learn about the differences, distinctions and similarities between spoken and written language, and develop sociolinguistic knowledge about language which enables and empowers them to switch between and across modes according to context, purpose and audience for language *use*.

What do teachers need to know?

What do teachers need to know about language which will help them and their pupils to acquire this capacity? What kind of classroom practices may assist us to promote acquisition of competence in and across spoken *and* written English?

First, general awareness needs to be established. Examples of such theory and practice abound in the LINC-produced *Looking Into Language, edited by* Bain *et al.* (1992). It involves helping pupils and students to see how written language is more permanent, more editable and more monologic whereas spoken language is more ephemeral, more dynamic and process-like and inevitably more dialogic. Second, more specific awareness can be generated by working on texts which display features of speakerly and writerly language in a wide range of contexts. The most suitable texts may be those which contain features of both spoken and written language forms. Good examples are provided by faxes, such as this example which has been slightly adapted from an authentic fax that a student of mine gave me a couple of years ago:

FROM: MIKE ROBERTSON
TO: JEAN–PIERRE
SUBJECT: MOTOROLA EQUIP

Hi!
We're on our way to Cantswell. One item I need your help with. We went back to Motorola and now have a tape for checking against Round Rock data. I will bring it to France with me tomorrow. Could you call/fax/E-mail Ken Barton and ask him to get us data for device D55A. It's a device fabbed on Oak Hill tell him. Either Fed Ex or datalink if possible. I'd like to do test Wednesday if we can. Thanks a lot. Call my car if you don't understand.

Here, grammatical forms such as:

1. One item I need your help with
2. We're

3. It's a device fabbed on Oak Hill tell him
4. Either Fed Ex or datalink if possible

are speakerly in that they display contractions ('We're'), deletion of main finite verb (4), and, according to written norms, have an unusual placement of object (1) and main imperative clause (3). Indeed faxes, electronic mail communications, and word-processed texts are altering before our very eyes the notion that written language is not process-like or dialogic and is not ephemeral.

More substantial examples are provided by advertisements which have the added advantage of often being interesting texts from the point of view of social and cultural practices, gender relations and the relationship between language and ideology. (For a fuller discussion of these particular dimensions, see Cook, 1992.) One example discussed by him is for Subaru cars. It is a written text but it has speakerly features:

1. 'mind you'/
   'what's more'/
   'which means'/
   are markedly spoken rather than written connectives.
2. several clauses are without main finite verbs
3. use of tags (e.g. don't you think?)

Such texts, as Cook points out, deliberately employ this kind of interpersonal grammar because they establish a dialogic and reciprocal texture to the text which suits its overall design of interesting and involving the reader.

A third stage, designed to deepen awareness of both form and function further, would be to compare examples such as those designed by Michael Halliday in his book *Spoken and Written Language* (Halliday, 1989).

Written	*Spoken*
Every previous visit had left me with a sense of the futility of further action on my part.	Whenever I'd visited there before, I'd ended up feeling that it would be futile if I tried to do anything more.
Violence changed the face of once peaceful Swiss cities.	The cities in Switzerland had once been peaceful, but they changed when people became violent.
Improvements in technology have reduced the risks and high costs associated with simultaneous installation.	Because the technology has improved it's less risky than it used to be when you install them at the same time, and it doesn't cost so much either.
Opinion in the colony greeted the promised change with enthusiasm.	The people in the colony rejoiced when it was promised that things would change in this way.

The sentences are invented examples (authentic ones would be preferable) but they can usefully exemplify particular tendencies in the construction of spoken and written grammars of English. Halliday points out that the example sentences with 'written' tendencies contain fewer clauses, have a greater lexical density and use more nouns and noun phrases including, by a process of nominalization, nouns formed from other parts of speech (e.g. *improve–improvement; violent–violence*). Thus, in the first sentence the 'spoken' sentence contains four separate clauses, more grammatical words (*I, if, that, to, there, it*) – as opposed to the greater number of lexical words in the written equivalent – but fewer nouns and noun phrases. Halliday claims that although written and spoken language are realizations of the same meaning potential (because the grammar encodes understanding of reality), they in fact offer different representations of reality. Since spoken language is focused on the clause, it represents a world of happenings, a dynamic view, a world of processes which is congruent with real experiences. Since written language is focused on nominal groups, where processes are represented as objects, it represents a world of things, a synoptic view, a world of products which conveys a metaphorical and therefore less direct representation of real experiences. It is worth noting in passing that many of the kinds of texts preferred as canonical (and indeed recently anthologized canonically in a British government anthology for secondary schools) are more writerly texts. Many of the texts preferred by teachers are more speakerly in texture. This can be illustrated by popular titles such as David McKee's *Not Now, Bernard* and *Come Away from the Water, Shirley!* and John Burningham's *Get off our Train* and the very interactive styles that the authors of such books generate in order to produce more *active* readers.

Speech in/and writing: a classroom example

The kinds of pupils' work to be discussed in this section arose from classroom work in which they first studied spoken/written differences and then written reports which differ in the audiences for which they are produced. The lessons involved explicit treatment of linguistic metalanguage, and also involved a classroom-based study of reports in different newspapers. Here are some comments about the writing task from the teacher of Claire and Sabina:

> As an experiment last year we studied differences between spoken and written language with all forms from the third year up . . . we're still learning the best ways of doing this but I'm convinced that a strategy of re-writing helps both the understanding and skills development of the kids. The re-writing with 3T also took the form of studying, recording, transcribing and then producing football commentaries as well as different written reports on the same match. There is more of a link than I had thought between studying something, modelling it for writing or speech purposes and getting effective language work from the kids. Sabina and Claire, who are avid Forest supporters by the way, produced several

drafts of their work using a word processor (with spellcheck) before they handed it in. I discussed some things explicitly with them especially their punctuation which they had really worked at, using basic terms like stress, rhythm and conjunction in a natural way, as the need for them arose. Sabina and Claire are probably the best two at English in their class, but the quality of their work and their enjoyment of re-writing procedures surprised me.

The result is two texts in which one is distinctly more writerly and the other distinctly more speakerly. Text A, in particular, raises questions for pupils themselves about:

1. the extent to which standard orthography can properly represent the spoken language
2. the extent to which punctuation rules follow grammatical patterns and how far they can represent the contours, rhythms and intonational patterns of the spoken voice
3. the extent to which Text A is more interactive, involving and reciprocal in the relationship it creates with its readers. It does, so, of course, at the expense of standard grammar.

MAN. UTD. V. NOTTS. FOREST

Text A

Man. Utd. 0 Nottingham Forest 3

Nottingham Forest are, back on the winning trail. A 3–0 victory over Manchester Utd. put a smile back on the Manager's face. Before the match Cloughie had said all the team needed was, a bit of luck. They'd worked hard all week they WERE playing like a team again. But, after they'd played a dull ten-minutes, Clough was out of the dug-out. What was it now? – another defeat on his mind?; another referee against him?; another fan on the pitch? He needn't have worried. On the twelfth minute, Nigel Clough – the Manager's son – put the ball in the net and turned to the bench and waved his fist in the air – all fired up? After that, the game stepped up and two more goals for Forest. One, a snap shot from twelve yards by Crosby; the second, a one-two between Carr and Pearce blasted into the roof of Manchester's net. After the match, Clough said: 'We got it right tonight'. And disappeared. S-M-I-L-I-N-G.

(Claire and Sabina 3T)

Text B

Manchester Utd. 0 Nottingham Forest 3

The flowing, fast football that Forest manager Brian Clough hoped his team would play, came back last night as his team had its first victory in seven games. Their 3–0 away defeat of Manchester Utd. was the result of a verbal lashing by Clough on the practice ground. He wanted them to show the skills shown before Christmas. Their teamwork was shown by a seven-man move which covered three-quarters of the field, resulting in the first goal from Nigel Clough, ever alert, from just outside the penalty area. By contrast, Manchester Utd. were disappointing. Their football was dull on a night which saw Forest shine.

(Claire and Sabina 3T)

Sabina and Claire show an impressive knowledge of how language varies along a continuum of written reports according to different intended readerships. Their knowledge of the different grammars of formal (closer to written) and informal (closer to spoken) is demonstrated in particular uses of language. For example:

Text A
- linkage is mainly by temporal conjunctions or adverbials (e.g. 'after that'; 'after the match')
- verbs are preferred to nouns
- adjectives are in a mainly predicative position
- clauses are mainly chained by conjunctions
- the text is lexically less dense than Text B.

Text B
- linkage occurs by lexical cohesion and by contrastive adjuncts (e.g. 'by contrast')
- nominalizations occur (e.g. 'victory'; 'result'; 'contrast'; 'defeat')
- there is more use of adjectives in an attributive position
- clauses are regularly elliptical and non-finite (e.g. 'shown before Christmas'; Nigel Clough, ever alert'; resulting in the first goal').

There are also vocabulary differences between the two texts with Text A exhibiting appropriately informal word choices. It is not always helpful to see spoken and written language in terms of polarities. The pupil's writing underlines what Deborah Tannen (1989) has termed 'the oral/literate continuum in discourse' – the overlaps and continuities that occur between speech and writing. This continuum is also sharply focused in the uses of punctuation, a point noted by Chafe (1986).

> Since intonation units are identified in the first instance by prosodic criteria (pitch contours and hesitations), and since written language is notoriously impoverished so far as its representation of prosody is concerned, we might wonder how anything analogous could appear in writing. Behind that question lies another that is more interesting; Do writers (and readers) have intonation in mind at all, or is written language a kind from which all prosodic features have been removed?

It is the overlaps and continuities between speech and writing which contribute to the different uses of punctuation in the two texts. In Text B the writers show a sound knowledge of some conventional rules of punctuation. In particular, the girls use commas effectively to mark off non-finite clauses (e.g. 'Nigel Clough, ever alert, . . .') and to signal the reflective 'pause' which occurs after an adversative adjunct placed at the beginning of a clause (e.g. 'By contrast,').

References to pauses indicates the close relationship between punctuation in writing and the representation in writing and the representation of speech. In Text A Claire and Sabina have produced a report which is markedly more interactive. This is done in a number of ways including question/answer sequences, quotation and a kind of creative indirect speech which takes the reader into the mind of the main protagonist (e.g. 'What was it now?'). Claire and Sabina attempt to involve the reader by using punctuation to try to mark suspenseful pauses, to stress individual words and to dramatize events. Such involvement is achieved by commas:

> Nottingham Forest are, back . . .
> . . . all the team needed was, a bit . . .
> But, . . .

as well as by capitals

> . . . and they WERE playing

and a playful invention with both grammar and punctuation:

> And disappeared.

and with word shaping:

> S-M-I-L-I-N-G

All these features indicate less attention to the content of the football match reports and more attention to interpersonal involvement. The girls make a fascinating effort to compensate for the contextual and prosodic impoverishment of writing and try to help the reader with the kind of temporal, spatial and logical relations which, in speaking, might be signalled more by the context, if not by prosody and gesture.

However, for the teacher there is a difficulty. Clearly some inventive uses of punctuation are more allowable than others. The play with word shape and capitalization might be fostered; but the placing of a comma between a main finite verb and a complement (i.e. 'Nottingham Forest are, back . . .') is too close a reproduction of the stress and rhythm of speech to be tolerated by the conventions of written language and offends against a *core* rule of written representation which it would be unduly relativistic to deny.

Pupils/students who are able to reflect on, comment on (analyse where necessary) and produce such texts are likely to be approaching a model of literacy which is rich, sensitive to contextual variation and genuinely functional. It is rich, in my view, because it above all recognizes and does not attempt to suppress the coexistence of spoken *and* written modes. See also Stubbs (1980, 1987): Hammond (1990); Perera (1990).

Conclusion

This chapter has focused on only one aspect of what we need to know in order to help our pupils know more about language and literacy. It is hoped that the focus on spoken and written language can, however, be read as symptomatic and as illustrative of the complex relationship between knowledge about language, on the part of teachers and students, and literacy skills. As with many areas of language knowledge we need to know more and to communicate that knowledge better outside a narrow professional audience. In our teaching we need to continue to explore the central functions of spoken and written language in society, to look more closely at language itself and in particular at the tendencies to privilege written language and grammars of writing in models of literacy.

> All the scholars whose work I have cited point out that literate traditions do not replace oral. Rather when literacy is introduced, the two are superimposed upon and intertwined with each other. Similarly no individual is 'oral' and 'literate'. Rather, people use devices associated with both traditions in various settings.
>
> (Tannen, 1982: 3–4)

We thus need to continue to describe and account for the more dynamic, interpersonal and reciprocal functions of spoken language grammars. We also need to continue to explore in our teaching the best ways in which to make such matters explicit for pupils and students so that they feed productively into enhanced skills in using language, the standard language in particular. And, above all, we have to learn better to challenge those outside who have much more limited knowledge than we do. But this is also best achieved if we learn to acknowledge and work with valid criticism of our practices. A disservice is done to everyone if it is said that nothing about our current practices should be changed.

Instead, the more we reflect on language and on the discourses of society which produce language and views of language the stronger our own frameworks become for analysing, supporting and developing our students' language and literacy. It requires, in spite of movements to the contrary, a constant recognition that language varies and changes, is always, with reference to its place in education, *contextual* and is best studied and developed in relation to real *texts*, not decontextualized or anaesthetized or invented examples. As Raymond Williams put it in his book *Marxism and Literature* (1977: 31) 'A definition of language is always, implicitly or explicitly, a definition of human beings in society.'

Pupils' and students' understandings of such properties and functions can only be properly supported by explicit contrasts and comparisons between standard and non-standard and between spoken and written forms. It has been argued in this paper that there are dangers if an overwhelming emphasis on standard English and on written versions of Standard English prevails and that the development of Knowledge about Language becomes non-comparative and non-contrastive, with notions of continua regarded as peripheral rather than central. But we should not be surprised by this since a main meaning of standard is uniform, and marching in uniform and standardized linguistic steps is part of a discourse of a national English language curriculum which, by the forces of its own establishment, has to deny variety and difference. A single, unchangeably correct, authoritative English grammar based on the proper formalities of the written word reinforces that establishment (see Crowley, 1989).

There are two final points to make; one theoretical, the other anecdotal.

1. It should not be forgotten that language changes through time and that grammars change too. They are subject to less rapid change than vocabulary but they change all the same. For example, the Gulf War of 1991 has made us all more aware of the finite nature of oil resources. Yet '*oil*' is a non-count noun (like water, air, petrol). The linguistic form encodes an implicit perception that such resources are unbounded and limitless. The twenty-first century may determine a change in the grammar when, as a result of diminishing resources, we may have to start talking about units of oil and petrol and – as they become finite – so the grammar may change to *count noun* forms such as 'an oil' or 'a petrol', or, indeed, to 'oils' and 'petrols'.

2. It is interesting to view a range of advertisements on British television and compare the uses they make of not only standard and non-standard grammars but also standard (i.e. Received Pronunciation or RP) and non-standard (i.e. non-RP) accents. Thus Standard English accents are used to sell banking and insurance policies, lean-cuisine ready meals, expensive liquors and exotic holidays; non-standard or, at least, regional accents are used to market beer (especially cider), holidays in inclement British coastal resorts and wholesome foods such as 'bootiful' turkeys from Norfolk and brown bread which is ('ot from 't'oven) or is invariably bread 'wi nowt taken out'. Given the connection between Standard English, proper accents, purity and cleanliness and the corresponding association of language variety with being unclean it is not surprising to learn that bleach is marketed with an RP accent. Dialects may co-exist with the marketing of 'Daz' but never with the marketing of 'Domestos'.

Examine in this regard the following quotation from Norman Tebbit during a BBC Radio 4 broadcast in 1985, in which proper Standard English is inextricably bound up with questions of social and cultural propriety:

> we've allowed so many standards to slip . . . teachers weren't bothering to teach kids to spell and to punctuate properly . . . if you allow standards to slip to the stage where good English is no better than bad English, where people turn up filthy . . . at school . . . all those things cause people to have no standards at all, and once you lose standards then there's no imperative to stay out of crime.

Few examples illustrate better, even if only anecdotally, the quotation from Mikhail Bakhtin, which heads this chapter, about the connection between social and cultural power and the homogenizing and purifying tendencies of a centralist and standardizing process in the formation of a national language. At the risk of repetitiveness, it is necessary to reassert the need for us all to interrogate such discourses and what they reveal about the continuities between spoken and written English. There is no more important area for teachers to know about in order to help our pupils and students to know about language and literacy.

3 English – caught in the crossfire

SEAN FARREN

Introduction

In his old age, the poet W. B. Yeats, pondering the possible effects of some of his works, wrote:

All that I have said and done
Now that I'm old and ill
Turns into a question till
I lie awake at night
And never get the answer right.
Did that play of mine send out
Certain men the English shot?

The Man and the Echo (*Last Poems, 1936–39*)

Yeats was remembering the executed leaders of the 1916 Easter Rising in Dublin, among them scholars and writers with whom he had been acquainted and over whom he feared he might have exercised some influence, leading them to engage in that ill-fated venture. I quote these lines, not because it would be agreed that Yeats actually had this influence, but because it is often perceived to be the case that in the Irish context, and probably in many other contexts as well, the words of poets, novelists and dramatists can have much more than a potential to entertain and intellectually challenge: they may also stir up old hatreds and provoke violence. Perhaps it was because of some sense of this potential that curriculum and syllabus planners minimized the study of most contemporary Irish authors in the curricula adopted for secondary schools in both parts of Ireland in the first four decades which followed the violent birth of the two Irish states in 1921–22.

In the South of Ireland, this may have been so because of a desire to cool the passions that had engulfed the state in the bitter civil war which had followed independence. So, despite the intense nationalism during this time, schoolchildren in the new Irish state in the period 1922–60 hardly made the acquaintance of any of the significant writers associated with the Anglo-Irish cultural renaissance which had flowered in the closing years of the nineteenth century, at least not through their English curricula.

In the North of Ireland, the exclusion of Irish writers was associated with a desire to strengthen the sense of Britishness which, in part, had motivated the region's majority population in its determination to retain the United Kingdom link and to resist incorporation into an independent all-Ireland state. So, like their Southern peers, most pupils in Northern Ireland were not provided with opportunities at school to become generally acquainted with writers of the Anglo-Irish tradition in the early decades of the state, nor indeed with any other significant aspects of Ireland's cultural heritage (Farren, 1976).

This situation did not change significantly until the 1970s and, at least in the case of Northern Ireland, it can hardly be claimed that denying access to Anglo-Irish literature had the effect of shielding society from the kind of influences that had worried Yeats. The violence and communal tensions which have characterized Northern Ireland over the past twenty years bear testimony to this. However, in an attempt to address this situation, educationists, among others, have begun the oftentimes painful process of examining the sets of beliefs, values, attitudes and perceptions which have driven the communities in Northern Ireland close to the abyss, if not quite over it.

In this chapter I propose to examine some of the principles developed and decisions taken by curriculum planners and which have been incorporated into the recent statutory reforms, especially as these affect the *Programmes of Study for English* (DENI, 1990).

A cultural corridor

In a recent article, Edna Longley (1993), Professor of English at Queen's University, Belfast, describes the cultural context in Northern Ireland as 'a corridor which nationalist and unionists vainly try to seal at either end'. Professor Longley argues that these two local political traditions, representing as they do age-old European conflicts over religion and nationhood have been vainly trying to seal off this corridor at either end from more recent external influences. However, to the extent that they *have* succeeded in sealing the corridor, both traditions have fuelled the tensions inherent in their mutual relationships and have minimized the potentially benign and developmental interaction with external traditions.

The corridor metaphor is a powerful spatial representation of the time-warp in which many perceive the communities in Northern Ireland to have been caught. Hence, it can be said that it has been to liberate present and future generations of young people from the snares and tensions within this corridor that curriculum planners have been devoting considerable attention over the past twenty years to curriculum renewal. Endorsing this aim, the Northern Ireland Curriculum Council (NICC, 1989a) stated that 'the tensions within "the community" in Northern Ireland underline the need for a systematic and unifying programme for young people'. In particular, the study of the cultural heritage of 'the community' in Northern Ireland is seen to be an essential element within that 'unifying programme' and while its effects are not expected, in the Curriculum Council's own words, to 'make Northern Ireland a haven of peace . . . [they] could do something to increase understanding at the same time as enriching pupils' experience at school'. The most dramatic curriculum initiative to implement this policy and with it the goal of more positive communal relationships has been the inclusion of two cross-curricular themes, one entitled *Cultural Heritage*, the other *Education for Mutual Understanding* as core requirements within all programmes of study for the compulsory curriculum.

Crossing the cultural divide: first attempts

The inclusion of these themes was preceded by a number of curriculum initiatives stretching back to the early 1970s. At secondary level, the first significant attempts to cross the politico-cultural divide were evidenced in two university based projects. The first was the *Schools' Curriculum Project* directed by John Malone at Queen's University, the second the *Schools' Cultural Studies Project* directed by Malcolm Skilbeck at the New University of Ulster.

The overall aim of the *Schools' Curriculum Project* was directed at strengthening the moral purposes of education (Malone and Crone, 1975) and to do so focused on promoting 'local studies' within the curriculum. The *Schools' Cultural Studies Project* was more ambitious both in terms of its aims, its nature and its scope. As Robinson (1981) states,

> the Project was an educationalist's response to the conflict in Northern Ireland and was concerned with increasing levels of tolerance, personal awareness and mutual understanding among young people in both controlled (Protestant or State) schools and maintained (Catholic) secondary intermediate schools (11–16 years), and, to a lesser extent, in primary schools (particularly 8–11 years).

So, like Malone's project, the *Cultural Studies Project* was ultimately concerned with values education.

Skilbeck (1976) argued that schools could assist in effecting the changes necessary to achieving a more open and tolerant society by seeing themselves as agencies 'for social amelioration, for cultural development, and for the support and strengthening of democratic processes in our beleaguered society'. The programme of cultural studies developed by his project was intended to promote these objectives by inviting teachers and pupils to acquire a critical understanding not just of their own and other cultures, but of the whole process of cultural evolution, of cultural identity and of the way in which people from different traditions perceive and relate to each other.

Evidence as to the success of such projects in achieving their declared goals is always difficult to measure. Nevertheless, Jenkins *et al.* (1980), in a report on the *Schools Cultural Studies Project*, pointed to what it regarded as 'the great success of the Project', namely, that 'it has got these sharp issues into the curriculum of Northern Ireland schools and it has produced many, many examples of courageous high risk and seemingly successful probing. In other words . . . there does seem to have been an unfreezing, an increased awareness'. Robinson (1981) points to further evidence of what may count as success, the results of a test of pupils' moral development. According to Robinson, the report on this test showed that the Project group of pupils

> more frequently and more consistently demonstrated a preference for high level or principled moral reasoning than did the control group which demonstrated a preference for items which reflected lower level conventional or even pre-conventional forms of moral reasoning, and it tentatively suggests that the experiences offered by the Project may have helped pupils towards developing empathy, understanding and tolerance.

Evidence was, therefore, accumulating from experimental curricular initiatives of apparently significant and positive changes in inter-communal perceptions, attitudes and behaviours. The result was that general lessons were drawn from these experiments as plans were laid for the reform of education which was to culminate in Northern Ireland's *Education Reform Order, 1989.*

Cultural Heritage: a cross-curricular approach

The first reference to the inclusion of Cultural Heritage and Education for Mutual Understanding as cross-curricular themes in the new Common Curriculum appeared in *Education Reform in Northern Ireland – the Way Forward* (DENI, 1988). In this document, the Department indicated that 'legislation will . . . provide that the curriculum of every pupil must contain certain educational themes . . . These themes will normally be taught on a cross-curricular basis, and the objectives within each theme will be incorporated into the programmes of study of appropriate subjects' (p. 6). Cultural Heritage and Education for Mutual Understanding were listed as two of six such themes and were prescribed for inclusion in programmes of study throughout the twelve years of compulsory schooling.

Education for Mutual Understanding was to be mainly concerned with encouraging contacts between schools of both communities and with providing opportunities for the mutual exploration of curricular and non-curricular issues. It was, therefore, essentially to focus on the contexts of learning from a community perspective. Cultural Heritage, on the other hand, was intended to remind teachers of all subjects of the need to develop an awareness and critical appreciation of the cultural heritage(s) which contributed to their particular disciplines. Because of its curricular focus, it is the latter which forms the basis for the discussion in the rest of this chapter.

The definition of culture contained in the Cultural Heritage Working Group's document (NICC, 1989b) is the well-established anthropological one which is stated as follows. '[Culture is] the artefacts, ideas, and learned behaviour which comprise people's way of life, and Cultural Heritage consists of those elements of culture which are inherited' (p. 17). The aims for the theme stress that pupils should acquire not just knowledge about cultural heritage, but the capacity to understand and evaluate that heritage, while the objectives emphasize developing an 'awareness of the shared, diverse and distinctive aspects of their cultural heritage' (p. 17). The scope of Cultural Heritage is clearly not intended to be confined to Northern Ireland, nor even to Ireland as a whole, or to Britain and Ireland. The scope is universal, or in the terms of the Working Group's report (p. 5), 'transnational'.

The transnational framework reflects the approaches which underlay the Malone and Skilbeck initiatives and, in Longley's terms, would represent an attempt to ensure interaction between local and external cultural influences. While all school subjects are included in this requirement, it is within the humanities, social sciences and creative arts that the most significant contributions to an understanding, appreciation and evaluation of cultural heritage are most likely to be made. This expectation is evident in the detailed set of objectives specified for the Cultural Heritage theme. These include, for example, pupils being required to

> observe, investigate and record shared, diverse and distinctive aspects of the way of life, past and present, of people in this region, the rest of Ireland and other parts of the British Isles. These should be explored through a range of artefacts, features, historical episodes, music, art, literature, pastimes, festivals, beliefs, customs and traditions . . . (pupils should) know and understand some international and transnational aspects of the evolution of their locality, of Northern Ireland, the rest of Ireland and the rest of the United Kingdom with particular reference to literature, music, art, religious beliefs, architecture, science and technology, movements of people, agricultural activity, economic trends and popular culture.
>
> (NICC, 1989b, pp. 17–18).

Since these objectives are now being required across the curriculum, it will no longer be possible for schools of either the Catholic, or Protestant community to avoid presenting each other's traditions to their pupils, or to avoid relating these traditions to wider contexts.

Cultural Heritage and English

As far as English is concerned, it is immediately obvious that Cultural Heritage can be readily accommodated. Indeed, as The 'Cox Report' (DES, 1989) points out, a 'cultural heritage' view of the English curriculum has been one of the defining approaches to the subject, while alongside there has also evolved a 'cultural analysis' approach. However, the former approach which 'emphasizes the responsibility of schools to lead children to an appreciation of those works of literature that have been widely regarded as amongst the finest in the language' (2.24) is not quite what is meant by the Cultural Heritage theme in the Northern Irish curriculum. Much closer is the 'cultural analysis' view which 'emphasizes the role of English in helping children towards a critical understanding of the world and cultural environment in which they live' (2.25).

In Northern Ireland, English is a fundamental part of the region's cultural heritage; it is a primary means for transmitting much of the region's heritage and it provides significant links with other expressions of culture, especially throughout the English speaking world. The Northern Ireland Curriculum Council's *Consultation Report on Cross-Curricular Themes* (NICC, 1989a) makes it clear that it is a 'cultural analysis' approach which is intended. For example, this report recommends that particular attention be paid to the spoken language in Northern Ireland, to the derivation of dialect words, to the influences on speech of 'Irish, Scots, American English and other languages from around the world' (p. 29); that pupils develop 'a critical awareness of how language can be manipulated to evoke certain reactions and appreciate how it can be used emotively' (p. 29). In their study of literature pupils are to be asked to 'analyse and evaluate critically a range of prose, drama and poetry from Northern Ireland including that which deals specifically with communal tensions within Northern Ireland . . . (and) relate the subject matter of works of literature to the social and historical environment in which they were written' (p. 29).

The possibility now exists for teachers to put the very language of communal tensions and communal politics as well as of government comment and policy under scrutiny, though the extent to which the invitation will be taken up remains to be seen. A much more likely outcome of these recommendations is an increased emphasis on the study of Northern Irish writers. Indeed many teachers claim that they have not needed the *Programmes of Study* to engage their pupils in such a study (Farren and Gray, 1993). The writings of Louis MacNeice, John Hewitt and Seamus Heaney among Northern Irish poets have been gaining increased attention in schools in line with their general reputation, while novelists such as Peter Carter, Joan Lingard and Catherine Sefton and Martin Waddell have been finding a wide readership over the past twenty years among 10–14 year olds. Perhaps more significant is the growing attention to autobiographical and fictional writing by Northern Irish writers such as John Boyd, John Harbinson, Michael McLaverty, Brian Moore, Polly Devlin, Bernard McLaverty and many others, all of whom reflect the impact of religious and political divisions on childhood and adolescence. All of these writers, directly or indirectly, pose immediately pertinent questions about the persistence of violence and the beliefs, values and attitudes which underlie it.

Consider, as a brief example, the potential in juxtaposing Hewitt's poem *Once Alien Here* with Heaney's *The Other Side*. Both poems reflect some of the general and everyday interactions and tensions between those who perceive themselves on different sides of the communal divide in Northern Ireland. Hewitt was of English, Protestant stock, a descendant of those who colonized the northern province of Ulster in the seventeenth century. His people display the determination and pride of colonizers everywhere as they place their imprint upon the land granted to them and introduce new customs, a new language and a new religion. In contrast, Heaney is of Gaelic, Irish and Catholic stock, a descendant of those whose lands were colonized and who behold with suspicion and some awe the strangers in their midst. Both poems are powerful statements of pride in one's own tradition, mixed with empathy, acceptance and respect for another:

Once alien here my father built their house,
claimed, drained, and gave the land the shapes of use,
and for their urgent labour grudged no more
than shuffled pennies from the hoarded store
of well-rubbed words that left their overtones
in the ripe England of the moulded downs
The sullen Irish limping to the hills
bore with them the enchantments and the spells
that in the clans' free days hung gay and rich
on every twig of every thorny hedge,
and gave the rain-pocked stone a meaning past
the blurred engraving of the fibrous frost.

So I, because of all the buried men
in Ulster clay, because of rock and glen
and mist and cloud and quality of air
as native in my thought as any here,
who now would seek a native mode to tell
out stubborn wisdom individual,
yet lacking skill in either scale of song,
the graver English, lyric Irish tongue,
must let this rich earth so enhance the blood
with steady pulse where now is plunging mood
till thought and image may, identified,
find easy voice to utter each aright.

I

Thigh-deep in sedge and marigolds
a neighbour laid his shadow
on the stream, vouching

'It's poor as Lazarus, that ground,'
and brushed away
among the shaken leafage:

I lay where his lea sloped
to meet our fallow,
nested on moss and rushes,

my ear swallowing
his fabulous, biblical dismissal,
that tongue of chosen people.

When he would stand like that
on the other side, white-haired,
swinging his blackthorn

at the marsh weeds,
he prophesied above our scraggy acres,
then turned away

towards his promised furrows
on the hill, a wake of pollen
drifting to our bank, next season's tares.

II

For days we would rehearse
each patriarchal dictum:
Lazarus, the Pharaoh, Solomon

and David and Goliath rolled
magnificently, like loads of hay
too big for our small lanes,

or faltered on a rut –
'Your side of the house, I believe,
hardly rule by the book at all.'

His brain was a whitewashed kitchen
Hung with texts, swept tidy
as the body o' the kirk.

III

Then sometimes when the rosary was
dragging mournfully on in the kitchen
we would hear his step round the gable

though not until after the litany
would the knock come to the door
and the casual whistle strike up

on the doorstep. 'A right-looking night'
he might say, 'I was dandering by
and says I, I might as well call.'

But now I stand behind him
in the dark yard, in the moan of prayers
he puts a hand in a pocket

or taps a little tune with the blackthorn
shyly, as if he were party to
lovemaking or a stranger's weeping.

Should I slip away, I wonder,
or go up and touch his shoulder
and talk about the weather

or the price of grass-seed?

Likelihood of success

English, along with other subjects but perhaps in ways more challenging, is, therefore, being required to openly address fundamental issues which touch on the very nature of communal relationships within and beyond the confines of Northern Ireland itself. It is being required to do so in a manner which implies something of Malone and Skilbeck's 'reconstructionist' views of education.

So, what is the likelihood of success? While there is much good-will (Farren and Gray, 1993), towards the cultural analysis and values education at the core of the initiative there are also problems, not least with one of the other basic aims associated with the theme, i.e. the extent to which cultural heritage will provide, in the Curriculum Council's words, a 'unifying programme for young people'. If within such a programme the initiative aims at deepening the understanding of different cultural traditions and at fostering respect for and acceptance of difference in terms compatible with democratic principles, there will be few concerns. However, if the phrase is intended to carry a deeper meaning, i.e. that the curriculum should unify young people *culturally*, it invites the question '"Unify" around what?' In Northern Ireland such a question immediately acquires a sinister connotation because of the fear that what could be intended is the cultural assimilation of one community by the other. Such fear would not be peculiar to Northern Ireland and, in the light of the country's cultural history, would not be difficult to understand (Lyons, 1979).

For example, within sections of the Unionist community fears have been expressed especially about the extent to which Gaelic culture might feature within the study of Culture Heritage. The Convenor of the Education Board of the Free Presbyterian Church, commenting on the proposals said

> If Protestant Children were to be taught the truth about these matters (Irish culture and history) we could welcome it. We believe there is a sad ignorance amongst Protestants on many things Irish. But it will not be the truth that the children will be taught.
>
> (*The Newsletter*, 14 June 1989)

A leading member of the Democratic Unionist Party argued that the proposals for Cultural Heritage amounted to an attempt to indoctrinate and called on parents to 'vigorously protest and remove children from these indoctrination sessions' (*The Newsletter*, 14 June 1989).

Knowing and understanding the culture of another community does not necessarily mean that pupils will cease to judge past and present events in a particular light, nor that they will cease to hold particular political aspirations, nor should there be any suggestion that they should. Pupils from a Protestant-Unionist background, for example, may come to know and understand more deeply the cultural traditions of their Catholic-Nationalist neighbours, but remain as staunch as ever in their convictions about the dangers to their own traditions from unification with the rest of Ireland. Similarly with the convictions of Catholic-Nationalist pupils. Pupils from both traditions may change such convictions and aspirations as a result of their study of cultural heritage, but any suggestion that that study should aim to unify pupils beyond providing them with a common framework and a broadly common set of curriculum experiences would be likely to be met with considerable opposition, as is evidenced in the comments above.

A significant initiative

The decision to include cultural heritage as a central theme within all subjects marks a major turning point in the history of curriculum policy in Northern Ireland. The situation has moved from one which avoided any significant interrogation of the local cultural environment to one which not only acknowledges that environment, but also poses fundamental questions about its impact on pupils' daily lives, their relationships, their beliefs, their values and their attitudes. In the case of English this shift is not one which will be satisfied by a mere passive exposure to the relevant literature; rather it is one which requires, on the part of *teachers* as well as pupils, an open, questioning and risk-taking engagement with the problems of identity and relationship raised by Hewitt, Heaney and so many other writers. So, by rendering the cultural heritage of all sections of Northern Ireland's society available to *all* its pupils, that heritage becomes the property of all, open to the critical appreciation of all. In becoming common property, it has the potential to promote respect and acceptance.

4 'Art made tongue-tied by authority'

PETER GRIFFITH

The school year 1992/3 was, to put it mildly, an interesting one for teachers of English in state maintained secondary schools in England and Wales. The government's Department for Education introduced national Key Stage Three testing (KS3) for these schools' 14 year-olds, and determined that the test results should form the basis of published league tables. It also decided upon a considerable change in the content and structure of the National Curriculum for English, abandoning a version which had commanded a reasonably favourable consensus within the profession. The combination of curriculum change by fiat and remarkably inept, and inapt, testing procedures provoked a strong backlash, and an effective boycott appeared imminent. Faced with this situation, the Secretary of State for Education carried out a partial retreat. This retreat, however, was too little and too late, and the tests proved a messy and embarrassing failure.

It is interesting to compare the attitudes towards league tables shown during this period by the Department for Education towards teachers and the Home Office towards the police. A draft Home Office circular, leaked to the press on 15 March 1993 (*The Guardian*, p. 22), warned of the dangers that pressure on police forces to achieve national targets could encourage officers to 'improve detection rates at all costs'. We could gloss this for teachers as 'maximize scores in Key Stage tests regardless of educational considerations'. Chief constables apparently feared that an attempt to rank-order police forces by crude measurements of performance would 'skew resources' away from 'difficult operations towards minor crimes which produce better detection and arrest rates'. We may perhaps regret that similar warnings were not heeded in respect of the English curriculum.

The larger campaign against testing has to be seen as part of the background against which the specific events relating to KS3 English were played out. Another part of this background has been the sustained campaign by right-wing think-tanks to simplify testing generally in order to increase its feasibility and to maximize its perceived objectivity and its actual pervasiveness. For advocates such as these, the pencil-and-paper simplicities of KS3 English were proof of its virtues as an exemplar and harbinger. In this respect, therefore, opposition to KS3 English testing must be differentiated from the wider campaign against existing tests, where a curious *ad hoc* alliance of left- and right-wing opinion was to be found mobilized, with results that were to become clear later in the summer.

No account would be complete without mentioning the background of moral panic against which this particular drama was played out. It requires no great insight to see parallels between the changes in the substantive content and associated examining methods that were pressed through by a Secretary of State for Education who had disengaged from any significant dialogue with the teaching force, and the contemporary comments by his Prime Minister that we should all look 'to understand less and condemn more.' The widely shared sense that this was a country teetering on the brink of irreversible economic collapse was simultaneously concentrated and displaced onto a more manageable concern about a perceived moral collapse among schoolchildren. English teaching was offered as a prophylactic against such a malaise – a corrective to the widespread consumption of TV violence that John Major had warned us about. To discourage random violence, 14 year-olds were to study *Julius Caesar* – though presumably they would not be set the death of Cinna the poet for detailed comment.

I will give an account of some of the techniques by which it was proposed to construct state-controlled testing of English in England and Wales, concentrating on the testing of Shakespeare. After that I will use work by Pierre Bourdieu to interpret some of these practices, before looking at one of the set Shakespeare texts for 14 year-olds, to see how it might be used for a different teaching strategy.

Initially, however, I want to consider how the pupils' own writing was to be examined. The KS3 examination paper was to start with a written stimulus, to 'help to set the context' (SEAC, 1993b: 4) for the writing task. The passages to be used for comprehension were to be distinguishable by genre, being 'narrative, descriptive, or discursive'. The third part, in which pupils were to produce their own writing, would require them to write 'with a clear purpose and audience in mind, for example to inform, persuade, or make enquiries' (p. 5).

The understanding of language functions which these instructions partially reflected was mirrored in the instructions provided for the compilation of the School Assessment Folder (SEAC, 1993a: 6). A *pro forma* had to be attached to each piece of work, to provide details 'such as the context in which the work was done, the task set, any help provided by the teacher', and the statements of attainment that were addressed. In a superb phrase, the document noted that 'Related teacher comments and notes of ephemeral evidence' were particularly crucial in interpreting whether the work consisted of student- or teacher-generated tasks.

Since these requirements may well represent important concessions wrung by colleagues from the 'punctuation and patriotism' brigade, it is important not be too patronizing about them. They provide an acknowledgement that language is socially situated, that language function determines or parallels language genre, that language users can attempt a number of differing performative acts, that language construction is variably constrained by differing power relationships, and, above all, that text and context are inextricably intertwined; terminology notwithstanding, 'ephemeral evidence' is not some form of optional diacritics, but is as essential to understanding the passage as 'the words themselves' are.

Well and good, but we are then entitled to ask why what is sauce for the KS3 goose is not sauce for the Swan of Avon; in other words, why the same understanding of language functions is not applied with equal rigour to that function of language that is labelled 'literature', thereby occupying the complementary part of the examination process.

We could indeed construct, in the interests of equity, the set of proper requirements that Shakespeare would have to meet before his own composition, entitled *A Midsummer Night's Dream*, could meet the examiners' gaze like those of the teenage examinees I am considering. He would have to state what texts had acted as a stimulus to his writing: had he perhaps been reading a passage from Ovid recently? Equally importantly, he would have to declare if he had written the piece on the off chance, or if he had been commissioned, or commanded, to produce it. He would be required to leave us in no doubt as to the context of the performance (just which noble wedding is being celebrated here?) and what effects his playtext was intended to work upon his audience or audiences. But these effects would not have been voluntarily chosen by the author. What guidance would have been provided by the commissioning patron, and of what kind were the relationships between the Shakespeares and the Stanley family? Clear answers would have to be securely attached to the playtext. 'Ephemeral documents' such as contracts specifying future productions at the Globe would also have to be appended. To make life easier for the candidate (a generous gesture on our part, considering that at 31 he was more than twice the age of the school pupils we are comparing him with) we should not require him to produce comparable sets of supplementary evidence for all the subsequent occasions throughout four centuries on which his work was to be performed.

In practice, the kinds of understanding of Shakespearian text that KS3 candidates were required to demonstrate were radically different from the portfolio I have just outlined. Since Shakespeare is clearly held to possess magical rather than rational virtues, it should be no surprise that the officially recognizable features to be observed in his plays form three magic triads. At first, we learn that questions will draw on a detailed understanding of 'plot, character, and dramatic effect' (Schools Examination and Assessment Council, 1993a: 8). A paragraph later, this has become 'character, setting, and plot' as manifested in a prescribed extract. A paragraph later again, an account of the question on 'the play as a whole' speaks of 'events, characters and themes'.

> Thrice to thine, and thrice to mine,
> And thrice again, to make up nine.
> Peace! The charm's wound up.

'Character' is the one term which is constant throughout the three triads – perhaps not altogether surprisingly, given the Bradleyan approach which is half-recollected here. I find the most depressing feature of the whole testing procedure, at a purely subjective level, is its uncanny resemblance to the 'Ordinary Level' exam papers in English for 16 year-olds I sat in 1957, and, even more depressingly, I suspect this is the compliment the testers would most wish for. Plot appears twice, and is even detectable within the narrow confines of a prescribed extract. Oddly, plot does not feature in a question on 'the play as a whole', though the 'events and themes' to be detected there may charitably be supposed to represent, in Aristotelian terms, the two component elements of plot. 'Setting' is to be perceived only within an extract, and as no further elucidation is offered it is unclear whether it refers to linguistic context or to stage setting. There is only one element which seems unambiguously extra-linguistic, and that is 'dramatic effect', of which candidates have to show a 'detailed understanding'.

'Dramatic effect' relates to the requirement that candidates 'show their understanding of the play as a drama to be performed, rather than simply as a written text' (SEAC, 1993a: 8). There is no further indication of what this 'understanding' may consist of, let alone of the ways in which both understanding and dramatic effect are socially generated and situationally variable. In their absence, 'dramatic effect' can only be something which inheres in the text, rather than something which arises out of the specifics of performance, with their necessarily variable interactions between stage and audience. That use of the term 'understanding' becomes something of a litany in the paragraphs from which I am quoting: there is to be a 'detailed understanding' of plot, character and dramatic effect, an 'overall understanding' of 'important aspects of the play', and an 'understanding and appreciation of Shakespeare's writing'.

Two further points need to be made. One is that 'Some questions set at the higher levels will ask pupils to comment on the differences between Shakespeare's language and modern English.' These questions, I think, offer us a guide as to what the earlier forms of 'understanding' were principally about: namely, the semantic content of the text, viewed first unproblematically, and then, at a 'higher level', philologically. The other point to be made is that, whereas such a question is a 'higher level' one, there were to be less able pupils – those entered for tiers 3–4 in the stratified examination process – who would not be troubled with questions about entire Shakespeare plays at all, since they were expressly forbidden to comment on these, even if they had studied them within the elective section of the syllabus. Their experience of what we are given to understand is the civilizing power of our greatest playwright would be derived instead from one extract included in a general anthology of literature hastily distributed to schools a few months before the examination.

As my guide to the educational and social stratification that I suspect KS3 testing willingly and intentionally sought to enact, I shall now use some of the work that Pierre Bourdieu has carried out in the fields of both education and aesthetics. I do so with some trepidation, because no-one has written more mordantly about the practice of academic citations and the other games that *homo academicus* plays. Using Bourdieu's own terms, and deploying concepts that he in turn took from Weber (and ultimately from mediaeval theology), he is about to be cast in the role of *auctor*, or initiator of ideas whose authority is self-generated, whereas I shall play the much more common role of *lector*, tending priest-like the sacred flame of his conferred authority. Finally, I shall introduce an ignis fatuus of my own.

There is a further difficulty in using Bourdieu's categories to illuminate this particular aspect of educational practice, and it is one that would apply to a significant number of other theorists as well. In a commendable attempt to avoid some of the cruder types of economistic reductionism, Bourdieu emphasizes the relative autonomy of various cultural fields, the literary and the educational being two. Yet in the course of literature teaching within schools, features of both are co-present, and I have tried to demonstrate earlier that in some ways the autonomy of the educational field in respect of the political is not so much relative as minimal.

Bourdieu is well aware of issues that arise from the co-presence of different fields, as his discussion of practice within the field of literary criticism makes clear. The validating of certain works, and the construction of a canon by means of them, is a process of exclusion more than of inclusion, and it is one that, through the strategy of concealing its power relations even from itself under the guise of aesthetic judgement, carries out what Bourdieu terms an act of symbolic violence. In the same way, symbolic violence is the very stuff of pedagogic action: 'All pedagogic action is, objectively, symbolic violence insofar as it is the imposition of a cultural arbitrary by an arbitrary power' (Bourdieu, 1977: 5).

But, as Bourdieu presents it, social reality consists not merely of fields of force, in which individuals are at best vectors of supra-individual forces; the field is populated by actors, each of whom undertakes behaviour that, at a conscious or unconscious level, is judged to optimize the actor's position within the field. Thus, actors within a specific cultural field trade on their cultural capital in order to maximize it; just as in the economic field, the best way to make a million is to start with at least half a million in the first place. The currency in which dealing takes place is specific to each field, and Bourdieu emphasizes that the literary field is in some ways the inverse of the economic in that the more recherché the product – and therefore the fewer the consumers to whom it is available – the more esteem accrues to the producer. Thus the writing of obscure but esteemed poetry pays cultural dividends in an inverse relationship to the economic benefits it generates; as Bourdieu puts it, the rules of this particular game say that it is the loser who wins.

However, in order to start trading, you need to have a disposition to trade, and you need to have some idea of how to gain access to the stock exchange. The disposition to trade is what Bourdieu terms the *habitus*, a set of assumptions and attitudes with which each individual is endowed by early formative experience. In Bourdieu's conception of things, the habitus, once formed, remains a relatively constant feature throughout an individual's life. The interaction of habitus and field tends to produce broadly similar results, field by field, in the case of each individual. Thus the teaching of a small canon, or even of some part of it, can generate patterns of taste in a constellation of related areas. There will then be a good correlation between those discouraged from theatre-going by their experience as 14 year-olds studying Shakespeare in classrooms, and the tendency on the part of the same people to avoid art galleries or museums during their future lives. Unless education functions in some way to reproduce the patterns of social behaviour between generations, Bourdieu argues, it is unlikely to be continued with. It must be on such grounds as these, then, that we must seek to explain what on the face of it is an extraordinary phenomenon – the mass teaching to late twentieth-century teenagers of a drama written as an occasional work to be performed at the house of an Elizabethan nobleman.

To attempt such an explanation, I want to look at *A Midsummer Night's Dream*, one of three plays from the short list of choices prescribed for KS3 testing for tiers 5–7 and 7–10 (average and more able pupils), the others being *Julius Caesar* and *Romeo and Juliet*, drawing on some of Bourdieu's theoretical points with a brutal kind of brevity.

Like other Shakespeare plays, *A Midsummer Night's Dream* has experienced a history of reception, reinterpretation, and sometimes creative violence that has pulled it in many different directions, from Mendelssohn's Germany to Cagney's Hollywood. This continuous process of reinterpretation, which Bourdieu would term misrecognition, has been particularly marked during my adult life. Recently I came across a reprint of Jan Kott's *Shakespeare our Contemporary* (1965), a book that I had not read for a quarter of a century, and was particularly struck by its characteristically 1960s depiction of sexual violence within the play – a violence that is viewed by Kott approvingly, or at best neutrally – as I had just been reading Terence Hawkes' recent *Meaning by Shakespeare* (1992), which plays a neat little five-finger exercise on the theme of sexual equality (very 1990s in its orientation) by affecting to believe that Nedar, the parent of one of the lovers, who is mentioned but who never appears, is just as likely to be a mother as a father.

My own reinterpretation of the play, perhaps slightly akin to Hawkes in its awareness of the rules it is breaking as well as of the rules it is observing, runs as follows. The underlying theme is the conjunction of the appearance of social mobility on the one hand with the reality of social stasis on the other; both are achieved by a process of education and of moderated and audited literary tests, which constitute the action of the play.

Most evidently it is the lovers who are educated and tested by the plot – and I say this not only because of the modern inflection that can be given to Theseus's address to Demetrius in the first scene: 'I have some private schooling for you both.' Private schooling of some kind they have undoubtedly had, as their glib displays of the fruits of a liberal education are designed to reveal. Lysander's avowed belief that 'the course of true love never did run smooth' is based on 'aught that I could ever read'. Helena's 'unnatural' pursuit of Demetrius is something that she interprets in literary terms: 'The story shall be changed/Apollo flies and Daphne holds the chase.' A grounding in Ovid is evidently the best preparation for an impending metamorphosis, since the lovers are able to represent their vicissitudes to themselves in and through literary terms. But this literary education is also a preparation for success at court, as is demonstrated in the fifth act; the lovers possess a *habitus* which strongly predisposes them to succeed in the field of power. To succeed, moreover, all that is required is to be a consumer (Demetrius tells us that he has 'come to my natural taste' on waking after the night's confusions); production is a task for others.

However, it is the mechanicals who more persistently and obviously see success in writing and performing as a means to turn themselves all into 'made men', and the failure of their aspiration to establish themselves as such constitutes the harsh comedy of the fifth act. Bourdieu's dictum, cited earlier, states that 'the loser wins'. The corollary of this is that a blatant attempt at winning, such as that which we see here, is by definition foredoomed to failure, at any rate with an audience that prides itself on the quality of its appreciation. The mechanicals' play is their own composition, and if we attended merely to frequency of occurrence we should judge that it was as rich in literary reference as was the lovers' discourse earlier; 'Not Shafalus to Procrus was more true' and so on. But these are references which are 'Extremely stretched and conned with cruel pain', not the fluent locutions that result from an expensive education. Bourdieu speaks of the differences between bourgeois and working-class French, and the varying effects they produce within an educational context, but the point is a broader one, and it is illuminating to apply it to the differing discourses of plebeians and patricians in this play:

> No-one acquires a language without thereby acquiring a *relation to language*. In cultural matters the manner of acquiring perpetuates itself in what is acquired, in the form of a certain manner of using the acquirement, the mode of acquisition itself expressing the objective relations between the social characteristics of the acquirer and the social quality of what is acquired.

And then a few lines later:

> The distinguished distance, prudent ease and contrived naturalness which are the foundations of every code of society manners are opposed to the

expressiveness or expressionism of working-class language, which manifests itself in the tendency to move from particular case to particular case.

(Bourdieu, 1977: 116)

As far as the mechanicals' play is concerned, the revisions that are incorporated during rehearsal, such as Bottom's reassurances to the ladies that the lion
is not real, are in the actors' own terms successful redraftings produced with
a specific audience in mind. The comedy of the situation arises from the
mechanicals' generous but misplaced assumption that their audience will lack
sufficient cultural capital in the field of the consumption of drama. When the
woodland rehearsal is interrupted by Bottom's transformation, the latter appears aware enough of the demands imposed by sponsored mobility (in this
case his adoption as a partner by Titania) to attempt a shift of register; he can,
as he tells us, 'gleek upon occasion'. What he in fact demonstrates, though, is
the 'expressiveness of working-class language, moving from particular case to
particular case' as he chaffs with the fairies or wishes for a bottle of hay. If
Titania had only been more aware of such sociolinguistic issues, one feels, her
verbal seduction of Bottom would have been more readily accomplished.

Later, of course, Bottom's half-recollection of the night's events is to be
written down and incorporated into the play. Like the good pupil envisaged by
KS3, he proposes to turn his experiences into a composition that will earn him
good marks. Like many more pupils, I fear, he is liable to be faulted for
insufficient 'understanding'.

The sad truth is, of course, that none of this literary effort will have any
effect. Theseus tells us, with the blunt realism of the self-confident ruler, that
poets are to be classed with lunatics and lovers as unreliable narrators whose
imaginations cloud their perceptions. When the Master of the Revels presents
a list of evening entertainments, it is instructive to note which are rejected and
why. 'The battle with the Centaurs' is a tale that Theseus has already told to
Hippolyta, and the narrating skills of a ruler are of course not to be challenged.
The death of Orpheus has been played before, and anyway the refusal of an
artist to perform upon demand can hardly be counted a fitting theme. Still
worse, of course, is the notion that women's demands upon a man should be
paramount in an entertainment destined for performance on a wedding night.
Worst of all, though, is the satire which is the last of the works that are
rejected:

The thrice three Muses mourning for the death
Of learning, late deceased in beggary.

Theseus claims that a satire is unfitting for a nuptial celebration, but we are
entitled to suspect that a complaint about a lack of state sponsorship of the arts
and humanities proved uncomfortable to him then – as it might to others
today. An amateur production, deploying limited linguistic and material resources, is chosen instead, since it can be despised while being patronized.
Theseus, it is clear, is no believer in the relative autonomy of art.

It is, then, important to realize that the interruptions by the noble audience which beset the players are not simply some separate but intercalated discourse, but are integral to the field of power in which actors and spectators hold a place. Bourdieu's way of making this point is a dense but rewarding one:

> The struggle in the field of cultural production over the imposition of the legitimate mode of cultural production is inseparable from the struggle within the dominant class . . . to impose the dominant principle of domination (that is to say, ultimately, the definition of human accomplishment).
>
> (Bourdieu, 1993: 41)

So, to find a new way to criticize *Pyramus and Thisbe* is to make operational a criterion of taste, to be tested according to that criterion, and in so doing to affect one's own position within the hierarchy of the court.

I hope what I have written indicates that a 'perverse' reading of the play can be made to work against the ostensible drift of what is for some of us only too familiar a text. Bourdieu's description of this type of subversive reinterpretation is that it is possible to 'get beyond' the dominant mode of thought and expression not by explicitly denouncing it but by repeating and reproducing it in a sociologically non-congruent context, which has the effect of rendering it incongruous or even absurd, simply by making it perceptible as 'the arbitrary convention it is' (Bourdieu, 1993: 31). It might be argued that to study a work of Elizabethan courtly culture in an unproblematic fashion in the classroom is already to achieve this effect, but this simple alienation is not in my view as fruitful as subversive reinterpretation can become.

To discuss the benefits of such a reinterpretation is not, of course, to argue that teachers should forthwith abandon their opposition to KS3 testing, or that pupils would be wise to entrust their futures to too ready or too overt an espousal of such an approach as the one I have outlined. *A Midsummer Night's Dream* may be a comedy, but the field of force of educational power is certainly no laughing matter. The pattern of classroom actions and responses is a significant part of it, as is the struggle between organized groups of teachers and the representatives of the state. Moreover, the teachers' victory in preventing exam-generated league tables in the summer of 1993 was more significant than anything that could be achieved by purely pedagogical strategies conducted in isolation.

There is nevertheless a significant irony in the fact that a powerful and determined intervention by government in the educational process should have selected as one of its chosen vehicles a text that lends itself so readily to the generation of an alternative set of meanings. The deeper irony is that these alternative meanings should be capable of providing so palpable an auto-critique, emphasizing the primacy of social class relations over the sometimes distinctly fragile autonomy of the literary field.

Bourdieu speaks of writers as the dominated fraction of the dominant class; a suitable modification of that formulation might profitably be applied to the role of classroom teachers within the structures of communication and control that function in the English classroom, and the struggles generated by the contradictions that ensue from these structures. To pose the question 'Who owns English?' is an attempt to understand the moves in those struggles. Like all real understandings, it can be a prelude to more effective participation.

5 Mother-tongue teaching in Israel and Britain

BERNARD HARRISON AND
AYA MARBACH

Devising language policies: background issues

The choice of language to be used in learning, and the choice of methods for teaching that language are, throughout the world, a politically laden issue. This is inevitably so, since language is the medium of knowledge and culture, and hence of power.

While countries may differ widely in their attitudes to 'who owns' the language for learning, we wish to argue on behalf of a universal principle for all mother tongues: that rigid distinctions between 'standard' (acceptable) and 'non-standard' (inferior) versions of language should be resisted, both on grounds of fair and equal opportunities for all, and on grounds of good strategies for language and learning development. While this may be a contentious view in many countries (for example, in the post-Education Reform Act phase of Britain in the 1990s), the principle deserves international recognition. Just as the international community has condemned apartheid on grounds of race as fundamentally objectionable, it might also recognize that to consign non-standard versions of a language to inferiority is to inflict a kind of linguistic apartheid on whole groups of people. Writing against divisive, 'Manichean' colonialist attitudes, Fanon (1968) identified 'intellectual alienation' as the product of

> any society that becomes rigidified in predetermined forms, forbidding all evolution, all gains, all progress, all discovery . . . a closed society in which life has no taste, in which the air is tainted, in which ideas and men are corrupt.
>
> (pp. 224–5)

It need not, of course be like this, and in many places it is not. There has, for example, been vigorous debate in the West Indies, about the status and potential of dialect language forms. Rohlehr (1989), writing about the 'troubled issue of the nexus between education, speech, class, status and power', showed how all-too-familiar views (for example, that dialect was a 'restricted code, incapable of expressing abstract ideas, sublimity or complexities of thought and feeling') have been challenged by the 'useful concept' of a 'continuum' stretching between Creole and standard English, from which speakers naturally selected registers of the language which were appropriate to particular contexts . . . If continuum theory revealed a potential for Creole as a language, the concept of an oral tradition made immediately accessible a virtually limitless range of prosodic, rhetorical and musical shapes, which inevitably become the basis of new making.

(pp. 1–2)

Rohlehr envisages a West Indian aesthetic which 'will embrace all ways of saying, all language registers' (p. 23), and which achieves both commonality and diversity of expression.

'Reclaiming our language heritage'

The title for this section is taken from Grace Nichols (1990: 283) where she, too, writes about her need to explore the 'constantly interacting' worlds of her native Creole and of Standard English. It was chosen in order to introduce attention to some key terms such as *confidence, ownership, empowerment* and *flexibility* in language and learning, especially where these concern acts of 'mediating between standard and non-standard, or between spoken and written forms of language. ('Mediating' is preferred here to 'translating', which implies the attempt to bridge incompatible language forms.)

In a study of positive attitudes to multilingualism, Harrison (1992: 37) recalled that, since there are thirty times as many languages as countries in the world, multilingual experience is the norm, not the exception, for most people. There is now a wide range of evidence to show that this common fact should be seen, not so much as a 'problem' in language and learning, but as a valuable resource, providing opportunities for enhanced powers of communication. Many problems concerning multilingualism in learning remain. These may, however, be experienced increasingly by those exclusively monolingual groups which cannot provide such access (see, for example, Cummins and Swain, 1986; Hakuta, 1986; Hamers and Blanc, 1989; Romaine, 1989).

It might, though, be argued that a requirement to mediate between vernacular and standard versions of the same language demands comparable skills to multilingual expertise; it is also likely to involve similar tensions (for example, in the clash of class and cultural attitudes). Such problems of translation or of mediation between languages, and between forms of the same language, should not be facilely dismissed. They involve, unavoidably, issues of power, equality, culture and opportunity, none of which may be easily resolved, whenever there is pressure to impose a 'dominant' language or dialect for educational, commercial or other reasons.

In a chapter on 'democratic' versus 'undemocratic' versions of national language policies, Devonish (1986: 35) urged that the everyday language used by ordinary members of a community 'is the most effective language medium for releasing creativity, initiative and productivity among the members of such a community'. This potential is, however, subverted by modern, centralized states which 'tend, by their very nature, to push official language policy in a centralized and undemocratic direction'. Devonish provided a range of examples (particularly from Third World countries) of how 'disglossias' (his term) are created by ruling groups, who then assume exclusive rights over the language of government.

A long-term solution, he suggests, might be for English to be a common world language (p. 40). He cites Jernudd's view (1981: 50) that 'the full development of local, national and regional languages may reciprocally liberate English for use as a truly international language' – though Jernudd adds a reservation, that its role remains tarnished by 'the misuse of English to prevent the economic, sociopolitical and cultural advancement of those who do not possess it'.

Claims for English as a universal language are, from one viewpoint, understandable. Walder (1992: 22) has pointed out that the number of people who speak some form of English as their mother tongue is estimated at between 300 and 400 million, and as many people again use English for daily purposes. From another point of view, however, only a small minority of people, even in Britain itself, will use Standard English as their only form of English. The huge international variety of English usage reflects a correspondingly huge diversity of social and cultural contexts, all of which require adaptations of the language for their particular purposes.

While supporting the principle of English as an international language, the African writer Chinua Achebe (1975) suggested that 'The price a world language must be prepared to pay is submission to many kinds of use . . . it will have to be a new English,' (in Walder, 1992: 26). Other writers and other communities have, of course, rejected English – because of its historic imperialist origins, or because indigenous languages better meet a nation's needs. For example, Hindi is widely used as a common language on the Indian subcontinent, along with English and other languages, to meet the needs for a common discourse of people with more than 1500 distinct languages and dialects among them.

Whatever the choice of a community or nation for a common language, the guiding principle must be that language policies should be aimed to release and empower people, to communicate in *their* community. Applying this principle to mother-tongue language teaching in schools, language policies must provide the powers of *flexibility* required to mediate between non-standard (usually colloquial) and standard (usually written) forms of the mother tongue. This flexibility is indeed similar to the kinds of flexibility required by all multilingual speakers; it releases a capacity for *intellectual*, as well as physical journeys, so long as *confidence* is maintained during the transition.

We suggested earlier that this principle has come under pressure in England and Wales, following the introduction, in all state-maintained schools, of a National Curriculum in 1988, with specified attainment targets in English (and with plans proposed in 1993 for further tightening). While Britain moves towards doctrinaire centralization, though, other nations, having been there already, are questioning whether an undue emphasis on language 'correctness', rather than on principles of flexibility, confidence and personal/community ownership of language, may not be causing actual harm to learning. In the light of this, we review evidence of the state of teaching the mother tongue in Israel, and some recent developments there.

Hebrew as a renewed language

In considering Israeli approaches to mother-tongue teaching, the unique history of modern Hebrew should be remembered. This distinguishes it from other 'natural' mother tongues, and deeply affects educational theory and practice. While the natural development of most languages is from spoken to written forms, the revival of modern Hebrew took an opposite direction – from the written to the spoken word. Ereel (1977) showed that, whereas 'natural' languages move away from literary standards, spoken Hebrew has moved *towards* written forms; the spoken language is now nearer to the written form than it was some decades previously. A century ago there were no mother-tongue speakers of Hebrew; the revival of the language since then, claimed Ereel, is the only complete sociolinguistic change of its kind known in history.

This remarkable phenomenon became a reality through the work of idealistic teachers in the early twentieth century. However, following the recognition of Hebrew as the language to be spoken and taught from primary school to university levels, education became centralized; this system has continued until present times.

Smilanksy (1972) criticized the Israeli centralized system, where the curriculum is prescribed by people outside schools, who assume an authority over the professional expertise of practising teachers. He argued that an externally imposed curriculum demonstrates mistrust of teachers, who are regarded merely as a channel between the prescribed curriculum and the pupils who receive it. The views of teachers are of no interest; they are not required to be critical, only to deliver the curriculum as required.

Tadmor (1989), a head of one of Israel's leading schools, invoked the ideas of Martin Buber, to make a strong plea for more imaginative leadership and open-mindedness in resisting conformist pressures from the centralized system. It might, then, be argued that, while critics of the Israeli system have highlighted its errors of central imposition, British educational policies in the 1980s and 1990s may have been in too much of a hurry to establish centralized control of the curriculum, of teacher education, and of educational finance.

Yet, while there have been pressures for change in the Hebrew language curriculum, the teaching remains controlled by notions of language planning which show no awareness of difference between spoken and written forms of language (see Marbach, 1991, for a full account of this). Ben-Hayyim (1953), in an influential essay, tried to address this issue by distinguishing between 'spoken Hebrew' and what he called 'cultural Hebrew'. The former corresponded, more or less, to the 'parole' of de Saussure, while the latter was the language of 'public' discourse in the media, or in school.

Ben Hayyim regarded language as a social creation, which can be directed, in the case of modern Hebrew, through regulation of 'cultural Hebrew'. He allowed, however, that 'spoken Hebrew' should develop freely, in ways which would eventually bring changes in 'cultural Hebrew': yet Israeli teachers have continued to intervene in their pupils' spoken language, disregarding any difference between spoken and 'cultural' (or standard) forms of language, in an exclusive concern for linguistic 'correctness'.

A similar gap between sociolinguistic theory and educational practice may, of course, be seen in Britain. Lyons (1981) pointed out that any linguist will, her/himself, carry the prejudices of a particular social, cultural and geographical background, and have entirely subjective notions of 'correct' speech. If we are honest, the speech that we correct in others is 'only incorrect relative to some standards which, for reasons of social prestige or educational advantage we wish children to adopt' (p. 83).

While this view may not be controversial in Britain (at least, among teachers of English) it is still disputable among Hebrew teachers, who see their task as imposing 'correct' (written) versions of the language on their pupils' speech. This may be seen as the ubiquitous experience of immigrant groups when confronting a new 'dominant' language, where parents feel pressed to imitate the versions of language that their children bring back from school. In such ways society controls speech, 'firstly by providing a set of norms, which we learn to follow . . . secondly society provides the motivation for adhering to these norms' (Hudson, 1980: 19).

In modern Hebrew, the set of controlling norms was based on classical Hebrew, and the motivation for adhering to them was based on notions of national and cultural identity. From a linguistic point of view, Hebrew was, until a century ago, only a 'langue' and not a 'parole' (to follow Saussure's terms). Yet it should not be assumed that the written form was a fixed, dead thing, unfertilized by the spoken form. As with all languages in use, Hebrew becomes subject to the (diachronic) influence of time, even though it may remain comparatively sheltered from geographical (synchronic) variations.

We turn now to *creative* aspects of language use and development, and of mediation, as revealed through the Hebrew experience, or through any experience of mediating between non-standard (colloquial) and standard (written) forms of language.

A new language for new realities

Speech, like writing, has its sedimented form on which all speakers rely for everyday usage. This is 'the opportune recollection of a pre-established sign', not the creative use of language which 'presents and frees the meaning captive in the thing' (Merleau-Ponty, 1974: 41–2). The Hebrew poet Bialik (1883–1934), who was a leading figure in the movement for the revival of Hebrew, did not differentiate between the written and spoken language, when he spoke of 'creating a word'. Preoccupied by the immense power of new forms of discourse, Bialik went beyond Saussurian notions of the arbitrariness of the sign or Ullman's (1962) version of 'transparent and opaque words'. He identified (Bialik, 1930) the relation between human experience and words as a process of 'covering and discovering in language', in terms which recall the thinking of such modernist Western writers as Pound, Fennellosa or T. S. Eliot (referring, for example, to the 'birth-pangs' or 'lightning-flashes' of new discourse).

Bialik's version of 'creating a word' may also be linked with an account by the West Indian poet Grace Nichols (1990: 283–4) of the 'battle with language' which is, for her, 'an act of spiritual survival'. She draws on the 'valid, vibrant language' of her childhood, West Indian Creole, in order to move her art forward into original statement:

> Difference, diversity and unpredictability make me tick.
> I have a natural fear of anything that tries to close in on me, whether it is an ideology or a group of people who feel that we should all think alike.
>
> (p. 284)

What happens, however, to the originality of a language, when that language has to be translated into another, or mediated between standard and non-standard forms? Even without translation, it has to be recognized that language and original thought do not always go easily hand in hand; in translation, the gap between arbitrary sign and what an individual 'really intends to say' becomes far more formidable. The barriers to communicating original feeling and thought that are set up by having to translate are explored with great effect by Brian Friel (1981) in his play *Translations*, where the British Army is conducting a first ordnance survey of Ireland, and working 'to translate the quaint, archaic tongue you people speak into the King's good English'. In this battleground between British pressure to standardize and Irish resistance to imposed meanings, 'Friel continually reveals humanity's need to communicate more than simple signposts through words' (Harrison and Mercer, 1992: 13).

Nida (1975) acknowledged that no translation can achieve the exact equivalent of meaning in the source language, since all acts of translation involve loss of information, addition of information and 'skewing' of information. Since there can be no absolute correspondence in translation, Nida argued, the translator should aim to 'produce in the receptor language the closest natural equivalent to the message of the source language, first in its meaning, and secondly in its style' (p. 33). To achieve this, Nida proposed a translation scheme based on the correspondence of grammar and semantics.

Gadamer (1966), however, chose a quite different approach. While also acknowledging that translation has no spatial dimension, 'that third dimension from which the original is built up in its range of meaning . . . no translation can replace the original' (p. 68), Gadamer insisted on the personal presence of the translator, who should learn to feel the intention of the original language, and transfer this accordingly. For Gadamer, translating was more a matter of what is termed 'Sprachgefuhl' in German (feeling for language), than of operating linguistic apparatus. In Friel's terms, he offers something of an antidote to the soldier Owen's view of Irish words, that 'where there's ambiguity, they'll be anglicised'. And, in terms of language and learning in education, Gadamer offers something of a freedom route for both learners and teachers, from the obsessions of government and establishment with standardization: of language, and then of thought and creativity.

Prescriptivism versus freedom in language and learning

The educational system in which teachers and learners work has, historically, varied considerably in British and Israeli schools. In Israel it has been a given context, where those involved have had little or no influence in determining policy, contents or methods of work; theirs is a centralized system. Until the 1988 Education Reform Act, claims such as that made by Stenhouse (1975) concerning the relative freedom of British teachers could be justified:

> The power of the British schools to define reality and knowledge is increased by the fact that in Britain the teacher is taken to be wise in deciding what his pupils shall learn and simply knowledgeable in teaching them what society has decided they should learn . . . Teachers have been rather free of policy constraints as compared, say, with Sweden, where most people would regard it as improper that curriculum should be with the teachers . . . The British system is well equipped to resist policies of indoctrination.
>
> (p. 43)

This relative freedom of British teachers was the subject of some envy abroad; Allen (1980: 15), for example, described how American teachers 'envied us our freedom from national, regional and local dictate'. By way of contrast, Smilansky (1972) criticized the Israeli centralized system, where the curriculum was prescribed (and even written) by people outside schools, who adhered to the view that there is always somebody out there who knows better than those inside schools; teachers were required only to comply, as efficient technicians.

As will be seen from the summary of evidence in the study below, the broad positions outlined by Stenhouse and Smilansky were still intact in the late 1980s.

The study

In the light of issues on the handling of standard and non-standard versions of the mother tongue in learning, the comparative study by Marbach (1991) of teaching in Britain and Israel found predictable divergences (and some unexpected similarities) of viewpoint, not only between Israeli and British teachers, but also among individual teachers within the same system. The study investigated teaching of the mother tongue in eight schools: four 11–16 or 11–18 year comprehensives in Britain, and four secondary schools in Israel. Teachers completed questionnaires; two teachers (including the head of department) in each school were interviewed and recorded, and an average of more than ten classroom sessions was observed and recorded in each school, across the 11–18 age range.

Most prominent, perhaps, among differing viewpoints were those on the standardization of language. A typical British view was:

> I try to set up a system which will allow teachers to bring in as many language experiences into the classroom as they can, and to produce as much variety as they can – spoken and written English – in the children. I do not see it as being defined in any narrow sort of way, that . . . the children use standard English dialect, or that I should coach them to get through the national examinations in English language.

> (Marbach, 1991: 311)

This familiar attitude among British teachers was, to a degree, even endorsed by the Kingman Report (DES, 1988), which received robust criticism at the time for its stuffy approach to the teaching of English. It, too, acknowledged that Standard English was developed from only 'one of the Middle English dialects . . . to become the written form, used by all writers of English, no matter what dialect area they came from. It is the fact of being in written form which establishes it as the standard' (p. 14). Other British teachers expressed views that:

> I accept non-standard language in drama work. I do not always correct pupils when they speak.

> I accept non-standard language only in special cases. I do not try to change their accent, but I want them to be aware that it is a dialect.

> I do not think that there is a 'standard language', yet it is important for pupils to understand what a dialect is.

> When I feel that children are confident enough, I correct their speech.

> (Marbach, 1991: 464–5)

While some British respondents revealed a confusion between dialects and regional accents (they viewed, for example, dialect variants as 'incorrect'), Israeli teachers were in no doubt about standards, or what constitutes correctness. The idea of a standard language for Hebrew is, after all, based on the fact that in a country where many children teach their parents the mother tongue, the spoken language has not yet acquired the stability necessary to create standards. Israeli modern Hebrew had to grow from the written form, and must be imitated by every new immigrant who wishes to be considered part of the nation. Thus the idea of 'mistakes' is based on deviation from the written standard Hebrew, without recourse to variant forms of the spoken language. This may change through time and usage; future speakers will make their own claims on the language, and it will be for them to decide whether 'mistakes' are incorporated into standard Hebrew. Meanwhile, Hebrew teachers correct pupil 'mistakes' according to the book.

The place of talk in learning

As expected, the study found notable differences of attitude between the British and the Israeli teachers, to the place of talk in learning. Less expected, however, was the evidence from the classroom observations that, despite large differences between Israel and Britain in theory and rhetoric about the value of talk in the classroom, there was little difference in practice. In the lessons observed, both in Britain and Israel, classroom discussion was mostly directed by the teachers. In Britain, only seven lessons were observed where pupils were encouraged to talk during the lesson; in Israel, only six – in all, 13 out of a total of 82 lesson sessions observed.

Neither in Britain nor in Israel were designated lessons observed where the declared objective was to encourage talking in its own right. This might seem astonishing to British educationists, given the influential work of teacher-researchers in this field such as Barnes (1969); Barnes and Todd (1977), Wilkinson (1975; 1982), Stubbs (1976, 1983) and many others. They laid the groundwork for the Cox Report (DES, 1989) to be able to pronounce with confidence that the profile component for oracy in the National Curriculum should be

> the development of pupils' understanding of the spoken word and the capacity to express themselves in a variety of speaking and listening activities, matching style and response to audience and purpose.
>
> (15, 8)

– although the Report then disclosed, in a note of coy trepidation, that 'we wish to stress that what we have suggested . . . treads some new ground' (15, 44).

Following his research into classroom talk, and more than a decade before the introduction of the National Curriculum, Barnes put these questions to teachers:

> Are they teaching their younger pupils to learn to accept factual material passively and reproduce it for matching against the teacher's model, to be judged right or wrong? Should they reconsider their use of full class or small group discussion?
>
> (Barnes and Todd, 1977: 27)

His finding, that teachers are not always aware of the fact that what they call class discussion is really their own talk with the participation of a few pupils, was confirmed in the Israel/Britain study. Barnes had, even earlier, drawn attention to the low level of pupils' sharing in class discussion, as a matter of educational urgency. He identified ways in which teachers may set up linguistic barriers between themselves and their pupils, which pupils were then expected to climb over, to reach the 'right' discourse and the 'right' answers. It is, however, 'only when they "try it out" in reciprocal exchanges, so that they modify the way they use language to organize reality, that they are able to find new functions in thinking and feeling' (Barnes, 1969: 61).

To conclude

Few have written more persuasively on issues of empowerment, relationship and dialogue in education than Martin Buber. He claimed that 'the relationship in education is pure dialogue', and that when the educator has made true contact with the learner, 'then that subterranean dialogic, that steady potential presence of the one to the other is established and endures' (1955: 98). Yet, while Buber is given an honoured place in Israeli educational thinking, his ideas are not reflected in established educational theory, nor applied there, any more than those of Barnes and fellow-thinkers in Britain.

Attaining high standards of knowledge is the principal aim of Israeli secondary schools, with ever-increasing pressure to achieve the highest possible grades. A great deal of knowledge must be transmitted during the few years of secondary education, and teaching is rigorously goal-orientated. All this has become increasingly familiar in the British scene, at a time when education has come under more critical scrutiny in Israel.

Under such pressures the teacher–pupil dialogue, in Buber's spirit, becomes marginal, so that education is relegated to instruction. We have sought to show, through critical reflection, and through the evidence of the Israel–Britain study, that attitudes to language, especially to the relationship between non-standard (colloquial) and standard forms, are closely tied to attitudes to knowledge itself, together with the sense of ownership and of power that knowledge brings. This is an international issue, affecting all languages, all communities and all educational systems. It is a political issue, concerning basic principles of human rights, and merits vigorous, high-level debate throughout the world.

6 Whose Spanish? Language and literature in the secondary school in Mexico

EVELYN ARIZPE

Reforms in any language

These reflections arise from my having been present in Mexico and in England at a time when reforms in the national curriculums of both countries were being proposed – particularly the reforms that have to do with teaching language and literature. In Mexico, these appeared in the Proposal for the National Programme for Language and Literature (*SEP*, 1991a and b) and in the National Agreement for the Modernization of Basic Education published in 1992 by the Ministry of Education, the *Secretaría de Educación Publíca* (*SEP*). For the last two years I have followed the debate about English teaching in England and Wales; my comments are based on the widely publicized debate in the public and professional domains.

My aim is to analyse what these reforms are really saying about the teaching of language and literature, whether in English or in Spanish. The following comparison is based on the *proposed* reforms, but I consider these are concrete enough to make some predictions as to how they will affect the teaching of this particular subject and the linguistic and literary experience of secondary school students.

In both Mexico and England we are talking about the possibility of one language and literature being made 'more equal than others': the 'official' language and literature imposed by the State on students who may have listened to, spoken, read and written other languages and literatures since they were born. There are not many differences between English and Mexican adolescents who have acquired a particular accent from their parents or the place where they live, who use and make up slang words with their peers, who flick through magazines and tabloids, watch television and videos (most of them in American

English) and who might have a different mother tongue, whether it be Swahili, Bengali or one of the indigenous Mexican languages such as Nahuatl or Totonaco. Confronting these adolescents with a language and literature that seem to have no relation to their own may impede a satisfying learning experience.

Education in Mexico since 1910

John Dewey wrote an essay called 'Mexico's Educational Renaissance' in 1926, when the country was in the process of restructuring itself, full of ambitions and good intentions, after the Revolution of 1910:

> I believe that the brightest spot in the Mexico of today is its educational activity. There is a vitality, energy, sacrificial devotion, the desire to put into operation what is best approved in contemporary theory, and above all, the will to use whatever is at hand.
>
> (Dewey, 1926: 205)

1926 was also the year that the official secondary school was established by President Calles, who had announced that one of his goals would be the development of public education.

Five years before, in 1921, the Ministry of Education was created by José Vasconcelos, one of Mexico's outstanding intellectual figures. At a time when 70 per cent of the country could not read, he is quoted as saying that 'If a country doesn't have anything to read, one had better leave it illiterate.' His efforts to promote literacy were linked to his aim to move away from positivist 'instruction' to a classical liberal 'education', and resulted in massive popular campaigns and cheap editions of universal literary works.

During this period the teaching of language became the key for national unity. Vasconcelos thought this would best be accomplished through access to great literary works; grammar books were completely excluded. A few years later, in 1925, grammars re-emerged and the main subjects became 'analogy, syntax, prosody and orthography', leading to learning based almost exclusively on fragmentation and memorization.

The unstable years between 1920 and 1940 were generally characterized by the attempt to impose a socialist education, where reason and science would have the dominant position. Education would ensure the continuity of revolutionary ideals through its role of raising class consciousness. Once the remaining indigenous population had been taught Spanish, the integration of the Mexican nation would be achieved. This attempt at socialism resulted in the Cristero War (1926–29) between the Church and the State and the deaths of some three hundred teachers. The references to socialism all but disappeared in the new constitution drawn up by President Cardenas at the end of the 1940s.

Because of nationalism, in the 1940s the Spanish class became the 'National

Language and Literature' class which focused on the Spanish spoken in Mexico, with a preference for Mexican authors and the introduction of elements of indigenous languages. By the end of the 1950s the emphasis on grammar began to decline in favour of reading and oral and written expression but, in the official workbooks, grammar exercises still predominated.

Since the 1950s, the most significant educational projects have focused on rural and higher education, national curriculum and official textbooks. In 1960, the first official textbooks were published and 100 million were distributed free to all primary schools. These have been the subject of much controversy since their appearance and they have frequently been attacked by both the left and the right: by the former for being too neutral and elitist, and by the latter (including the Catholic Church) for, among other things, being too socialist and popular. The textbooks were re-edited in the 1970s and 'structural linguistics' were introduced. Twenty years later, it has been decided to exclude this topic from the new programme and textbooks.

This century has seen the rapid development of education in Mexico since the Revolution, but the changes in the teaching of language and literature show the incongruities within the system. Since Vasconcelos, a succession of thirty ministers has occupied his post and the string of inconsistent policies and unfinished projects they have left behind have greatly affected progress.

The present: teaching language and literature

The major changes in the Spanish curriculum for secondary education in the last twenty years occurred in 1974, in 1981 and in 1992. The first was to move the central focus of the programme from literature from Spain to literature from Mexico and Latin America. The second was to divide the Spanish programme for each of the three years of secondary education into eight units. Each unit has objectives for the same aspects that are studied in primary Spanish: oral expression, written expression, reading, literature and notions of linguistics.

The Ministry of Education does not provide an official textbook for secondary like it does for primary. Primary school children receive an anthology of traditional verse, tales and legends, poems and short stories written by contemporary authors for children, as well as abridged versions or fragments of world literature. There is also an accompanying workbook for practising grammar, linguistics, phonology, spelling and writing. Secondary school children must buy one of the privately written textbooks approved by the SEP authorities. These textbooks contain the literary texts which are to be read during these three years and are intended to provide an historical view of world literature. They also contain exercises and suggestions for class activities.

One of these textbooks is called *Español activo* (Lozano, 1991). It was first published in 1977 and is still used in most government and private schools. In each of the eight chapters there is a brief introduction in which authors' social

and historical contexts are described and which includes summarized characteristics of the literature of the period. A brief biography of the authors may be
given and then a fragment of a selected text, in the case of a novel, or the
complete short story, poem or play.

For Year 7 there are no prescribed texts. The teacher can choose simple
texts that allow students to identify aspects such as characters, theme, poetic
images, rhythm and meter and to compose summaries and paraphrases. For
Year 8, the texts range from 'ancient classical literature' (China, India, Greece,
Rome, Egypt, pre-hispanic Mexico) through mediaeval and renaissance texts,
to neoclassical literature. Year 9 students are expected to read texts from the
baroque, romantic, realist and modernist periods and end the course with
samples from twentieth-century poetry, narrative and drama.

The activities that accompany the reading include:

- explaining the content in a class or group discussion
- pointing out the characteristics of the text, its historic period, genre, theme,
  plot, characters, setting
- identifying figures of speech (metaphors, comparisons, poetic images)
- doing exercises on the identification and correct use of verbal tenses and
  parts of speech
- summarizing the main characteristics of the period or genre
- creating a literary album or classroom display with poems and author's
  biographies, writing an essay or a poem, performing a short drama.

It is clear that the objectives and the activities exemplified above correspond
to a view of literature in which the author and the context are more important
than the text itself, except when the text is used to illustrate linguistic aspects.
In the first place, the texts are usually not read in their complete versions, but
as fragments, so there is no idea of the text as a whole. Each text is intended
to represent an author, a genre and a given period according to its intrinsic
characteristics. This practice creates the illusion of a universal body of literature
that can be neatly labelled. It reduces the complex process of literary production
to a series of dates (to be memorized) that are vaguely related to historical,
social and political events, and it supports a limited list of 'masterpieces',
written by 'great' authors of unquestionable merit.

Reading becomes an activity in which the readers must search for clues that
allow them to place the text in its context, but with little comprehension or
enjoyment. This is the extent to which it can be said that the readers participate
in the text, because there is no room for them personally in the formulaic
author-(text)-context/literary period relationship that persists throughout the
programme. The students are limited to finding and selecting information and
are not encouraged to understand, analyse and interpret as responsive readers,
even though these are supposed to be the objectives of the Spanish programme.

Each teacher follows the textbook and has limited freedom to decide how to
achieve the objectives expected by the programme. Usually, the main concern

is to cover the programme in order to prepare students for the set test. Assessment takes the form of four examinations a year, set by the Ministry of Education, which refer to the texts on the curriculum and also contain questions (mostly multiple choice) on grammar and vocabulary. Preparing for these tests leaves little or no room for a dialogue between the teacher and the student or among the students themselves. Natural language abilities are not exploited and pupils are forced into an almost predetermined response in order to accomplish the ambitious objectives of the programme. While some teachers use a variety of more creative strategies that involve the students, most use what they know has worked before and that keeps the class under control. Lack of resources, beginning with the lack of books other than the textbook, is also a major constraint in the Spanish class.

In short, although the National Curriculum for Spanish states that language and literature should be *appreciated* as forms of art, they are really being used as educational tools: useful instruments for communicating, for obtaining information and for acquiring 'culture'.

The future: the modernized Spanish programme

The programme developed for Spanish in the 1992 educational reform apparently intends to change the traditional view of literature by emphasizing student participation, focusing on reading and writing rather than linguistics and allowing more flexibility in the selection of texts. The *Modernized Programme* for secondary is divided into three aspects: 'Functional Communication', 'Literary Communication' and 'Literary Culture'. The first proposes to make the student more efficient in understanding a text and more precise in writing one. The second intends to promote the creation of personal texts through reading literary texts and writing experimentally. The third involves selecting texts that belong to a certain period in literary history and studying them in such a way that the student will 'know, appreciate, enjoy and value' each text.

Like the previous programme, the study of these texts includes paraphrasing, locating the primary and secondary ideas, recognizing figures of speech and, according to these characteristics, locating the texts within a literary period. The only major difference is that it eliminates grammar exercises and the general focus is meant to be on the emotive content of the texts and what this content means to individual students. The analysis of a text is meant to be 'logical and interpretational' instead of merely historical. What this and other such terms mean, though, is left unclear.

The modified programme claims more flexibility in the selection of texts, but the list has simply been expanded (for Years 8 and 9 it now includes English authors such as Shakespeare, Milton and Dickens), and there is no mention of texts that do not fit into this canon of 'world literature'. Although there is less emphasis on the author and his context, it will be interesting to see if teachers are going to abandon the practice of asking for biographies. The way in which the students will be evaluated is also unclear, although the general idea is that they will present a term paper at the end of the year that is a culmination of all their previous exercises.

While the new programme takes some steps in the direction of a more reader-orientated approach to literature, encouraging the students to express their feelings orally and in writing, and excluding the useless linguistic exercises, the principles that underlie it have not changed. In particular, the view of language as an instrument for communicating 'functionally' and the view of literature as a vehicle for the transmission of a cultural heritage have been retained.

Deciding whose language and literature

I have described the situation in Mexico in order to draw some parallels with that in England. Although there are obvious differences, there seems to be a similar general trend in the education projects for both countries. This trend is not always explicit: in fact, at least in Mexico, there seems to be an effort to hide it under confusing but formal-sounding names. Throughout the following list of observations I will try to point out how some of the patterns in the new carpets have been designed to conceal the dirt more effectively. There are other aspects, but I will restrict myself to eight main points.

1. There is a similar view in both countries about the reason for teaching language and literature. In England, the reforms favour a traditional 'moral and cultural values' model. They reject the personal growth or 'self-discovery' model popular in the last twenty years and do not take into account the contemporary version of this model that many teachers believe in, that is, a model of personal growth within a social context that is related to the whole curriculum. In Mexico, the model of 'moral, cultural and aesthetic values' promoted by a romantic nationalist attitude (a legacy from the Vasconcelos' period), persists throughout the new programme:

> There is no doubt about the virtues of a programme based on reading . . . to overtake the limits of the word and unearth the mysterious and infinite worlds of man as creator. It is considered that reading is the best way of acquiring culture with the aim of organizing it in coherent units of interrelated [universal] values.
>
> (*SEP*, 1991a: 7)

There is no reference at all to the value of the individual learning about literature and language in order to develop a critical awareness of the relationship between 'the word and the world'.

2. In Mexico, the authors of previous Spanish textbooks for primary were notable left-wing academics. None of them was consulted when the new textbooks and programmes were written. This seems to parallel the situation in

England where the government has tended to subscribe to the belief that research and teaching have fallen into the hands of left-wing ideologues and that it has been its duty to rescue it. Others believe that the current reforms of teaching English in England and Wales are not so much concerned with educating as with preaching a rival, right-wing ideology. As a result, teachers and researchers in both countries have been 'left out', planning has gone on behind closed doors without taking their previous experience, either positive or negative, into account, and the reform has been presented as a *fait accompli*.

3. In both countries the reforms seek a return to 'basics'. In Mexico, these are taken to mean reading, writing and speaking as opposed to grammar and linguistics. In England, the basics are considered to be reading and writing, with a focus on grammar, spelling and listening as opposed to personal response and knowledge about language. Both cases seem to be a swing of the pendulum in the old dispute about the place of grammar in the curriculum. I see all these skills as having a place in the curriculum: the problem is when memorization, repetition and mechanical skills are given priority over analysis and dialogue. What seems more debatable is the focus on language only as a tool for efficient communication, not as a means for creative expression, reflection and empowerment.

4. A similar mechanistic view of working with language is proposed for literary texts in the Mexican programme. The aim is to have students match texts to a period in literary history. They must identify central themes, main characters, and describe plots. They must also recognize comparisons, metaphors, rhyme and meter. But there is no mention of studying the historical, social and even political significance of these aspects, of discussing them in the light of the author's intention and of the reader's response. This traditional critical method leads to what Louise Rosenblatt (1982) calls an 'efferent' reading stance, reading for information to answer factual questions about the text or to summarize it. It does not encourage an 'aesthetic' reading in which a deeper and more personal response arises from a pleasurable experience.

5. In both countries there is a list of prescribed texts, or 'canon'. In Mexico, this list has been widened to provide more choice, but it is still composed of recognized 'great literature'. In England, the list has been narrowed down and most of the wealth of English literature for children and adolescents has not been mentioned; nor has much literature in English by non-British writers. Nowhere in the curriculum is there an officially recognized space for foreign literature in translation: it is as if it simply did not exist. In the Mexican anthologies and in the English government's assessment English anthology for pupils aged 14 (DFE, 1993) the texts are presented out of context and sometimes in abridged fragments. This issue has been best summarized by Otto (1992–93: 320) in a recent column in *Journal of Reading*: 'Where there is a perceived need to fight about the canon, the battle has already been lost.' He implies that behind the move to impose a canon there is already the assumption that if a book does not become a prescribed text, it will probably never be read.

6. Regarding assessment, in Mexico the proposal is not yet clear, but it suggests a move away from closed questions to examining progress through individual and group term projects. In England the move is back to assessment based on questions which assume acceptable and unacceptable readings of a text. It is a monosemic view of literature which demands that all students converge towards the same interpretation of the text.

7. In Mexico, with the many unresolved problems that teachers already face, such as a huge workload and meagre salary, the continuous changes which they are expected to make and in which they have had no say are simply a small pain. Most teachers are used to stepping around whatever the new minister comes up with, and quietly continue teaching as they always have. In England, the events seem to be setting up a similar situation and, if teachers are not allowed a space for using their own initiative and judgement, no matter how closely they are monitored, I can imagine a similar form of resistance will be forthcoming.

8. In both countries, the reforms have been legitimized by reference to the negative results of the previous curriculum, but without any reference to a concrete body of educational research. The Mexican modernization project does not mention educational research at all and seems to believe that the everyday experience of teachers will be enough to resolve any problems or queries. Although little research has been done on Spanish teaching, this does not mean it is non-existent. In England, on the other hand, there is a substantial body of intelligent research on all aspects of English teaching, but this has evidently been ignored whenever it might challenge the new orthodoxy. The assumption that seems to lie beneath this attitude is that in a programme directly dictated by the government, expert research is unnecessary and superfluous.

What influence will these reforms have on the students' experience of language and literature in school? My prediction is that most adolescents will feel alienated, bored and frustrated. In Mexico, what students read outside school is ignored to the extent that it is not even an issue in the Spanish class whether street language, popular novels or comic strips should have a place in the curriculum. The assumption is that these are not part of 'real' language and literature; the result is a polarization of elite and mass culture. The same may well apply in England. Once students feel alienated from what is academically and socially regarded as 'real' culture – because they do not possess the 'codes' necessary to decipher it – then their expectations about any other cultural activities will also be curtailed.

One of the major criticisms that have been made of the new Mexican model is perhaps the key to interpreting the general trend in teaching language and literature in both countries. This has to do with the way in which the question of power has been resolved. Throughout the Mexican documents on the reforms, there are constant allusions to the right of students, teachers and researchers to *participate* in the new model of education, but, there is no mention of their right to *decide*. Although there are differences in the degrees of participation in both countries, the point is that any participation allowed to students as well as to teachers and researchers will always be *within the context that others have chosen for them*. The question of 'Whose English?' or 'Whose Spanish?' is inextricably linked to questions to do with knowledge and control: Who is really deciding, for whom and what for?

7 English as a multiform medium

P. V. DHAMIJA

English is used as a native language in five countries, and as a non-native second or foreign language in about sixty others. The total number of users may amount to something like 700 million (Kachru, 1992). In view of its spread and use, it may be regarded as the most widely used language in the world. Since privilege entails responsibility, it has taken upon itself the duties of doing many things for many people. In order to discharge these duties, it has expanded and developed enormously, thus varying its form and function and becoming one of the fittest communicative mediums for a large variety of societal and intersocietal communicational needs. In what follows, I reflect upon some of the functions that English as a medium has been performing.

English as a link language

English today is a global link language *par excellence*. Almost every country in the world communicates with another through English, quite often even with its close neighbours. India is a notable example. If an Indian has to communicate with a German, a Frenchman, a Russian, or a Spaniard without the aid of an interpreter, the best bet would be in English.

Within the Commonwealth countries, and groups of countries, such as India, East Africa, West Africa and Central Africa, the main link language among the different linguistic regions and communities is English. In all these countries, especially in India, the colonial hang-over has generated a strong bias in favour of English, which is supported with funds and propaganda administered by the British Council and American foundations located there. Moreover, the universal love of the exotic has nurtured an English snobbery, which may take quite some time to mellow into a tolerable species of it.

The upshot is that English is perhaps the most powerful link language in the world. The shrinking of the globe is due as much to this communicative link as to the communication links provided by supersonic aviation and telecommunication.

English as a medium of literary creativity

The volume of literature written in English today is enormous and comparable with the best written in any one language or regional groups of languages. This point is not easy to research. However, if one makes a sample survey of the publications appearing in a limited period, one can make a fairly reliable statement of the ratio of the literature written in English to that written in any one of the major world languages. I have attempted such a survey. I focused on five years, from 1980 to 1985, and computed literary publications from *Books in Print* and *Articles in Print* for five major world languages: English, French, German, Russian and Spanish. The figures are:

English	21 257
French	13 358
German	12 459
Russian	14 110
Spanish	9 599

I must add here that most literary and critical works of note are translated into English at the earliest opportunity. In fact, English is often one of the first few languages into which any literary creation or critical work is translated. The reason may simply relate to the number of consumers, but this would not detract from the importance of English as a repository of any literature.

An important point is the use of English in literatures written in the Commonwealth countries. Among the outstanding examples are the Indo-Anglian and African literatures written in English and in which English has been stretched, it seems, to its highest creative potential in that it has had to express varied experiences alien to its genius. For instance, one could look at any few pages from Raja Rao's *Kanthapura* (1938), or Achebe's *Arrow of God* (1964), or Ngugi's *The River Between* (1965), or from any one of Wole Soyinka's novels or plays. The typical Anglo-American attitude to these literatures is too well known, to my mind, to need any documentation. At worst, it is condescension of a rather disheartening kind. It could be traced to a general native speaker's dislike of the use of English in these literatures. Perhaps such a critic finds his language violently twisted and distorted. But it is precisely this 'distortion' which is the very *sine qua non* of these works. The medium has had to be made malleable enough to adapt to the demands of the 'foreign' cultures, which craved for expression. Any language is basically culture-bound, and to attempt to cast a particular culture in the mould of an alien language would be a tremendous task. Yet, English has been made hospitable to Indian, African and Caribbean cultures. It has absorbed masses of native vocabularies and expanded its morphological potential to the full to meet the challenge of depicting these cultures. In other words, English has been 'nativized' to a remarkable degree to accommodate them. And English has been somewhat nativized for certain other important purposes as well – for instance to be a fit vehicle for intra-state communication, business and administration in these countries.

English as a medium of science and technology

No language is a more suitable vehicle for scientific and technological research and purveyance. Currently, more than 50 per cent of the research papers on physical sciences are published in English. The remaining papers are available in English translation across the world. So, if you know English, you have direct access to this enormous source of information. The story of technology is also more or less the same. Most of whatever is not copyrighted and mono-polized, and is magnanimously thrown open for the benefit of mankind at large, is available in English – either in original or in translation. Indeed, it would not be an exaggeration to say that if you have no English, you may have no access, or only delayed access, to this enormous reservoir of human knowledge.

English as a language of reference and research

The use of English as a medium of reference and research is universal. No library in the world today has a collection which excludes books and journals in English, and even on English. There may be many small libraries in any country not having among its collection a single book or journal in French, German, Russian or Spanish, but a library without books and journals in English is inconceivable. In any research-orientated library, reference materials are invariably available in English. An important belief popular among some teachers of English in North India is that if you know English, you know every language in the world. The exaggeration is obvious, but the fact remains that through English you have access, sooner or later, to anything worth reading published in any language.

The use of English in India

What we have said about English above generally applies to most other Com-monwealth countries. But two ways in which the use of English is peculiar to India are as a medium of instruction, and as a source language.

In the countries of the Indian subcontinent, English is used as a medium of instruction at all levels of education, but I must add a caveat here. English is not used as a medium of instruction in all schools, colleges and universities. There are at least two clearly distinguishable streams of education – the elitist and the non-elitist. In the first stream, instruction in English begins the day a pupil joins school. As soon as he has learnt his Roman alphabet and can read and write (i.e. pronounce, copy, take dictation, and so on), he begins his 'general studies', including history, geography, civics, through the medium of

English, and his unending task of memorizing or cramming begins. English will be his medium of instruction as long as his education lasts. Thus, for this stream of 'privileged' learners, the medium of instruction is English from their kindergarten right up to the last stage in their higher education.

For the non-elitist stream, on the other hand, English is not an obligatory language of instruction at the primary and the secondary levels of education. Learners can opt for instruction in English at the secondary level, but in fact, not even 1 per cent of them receives it in English. At the tertiary level, the scene is qualitatively different. There are not enough English-medium institutions of higher learning for the elitist groups of learners, who have had a kind of exclusive education in their 'English-medium cloisters'. Consequently, the majority of them have to share their desks with their 'lowbrow' brethren in the tertiary classroom. In such classrooms, the medium of instruction is a sort of combination between the learners' first or regional language and English. However, the majority of the institutions at the tertiary level, especially those located in semi-urban and rural areas, impart instruction in the relevant regional language. English is used only for reference or resource when textbooks or materials on certain required topics or subjects listed in the curriculum are not available in the regional language. In the Hindi-speaking states, for instance, Hindi is the medium of instruction, and English a resource language. In a few institutions of higher education, mainly English is used as a medium of instruction. Such institutions are a few 'autonomous' colleges largely in the Southern states, a hundred odd institutes of specialized technical education, ten central universities and a few Civil and Defence training colleges.

The three-medium system of higher education outlined above seems to be a fortuitous development in that it has not resulted from any systematic execution of any national plan or policy. The formulation of language policy, particularly with regard to the medium of instruction, in post-Independence India has not been consistent. This stems from a disquieting degree of ambivalence which is clearly discernible from a chronological examination of the recommendations of Education Commissions and Committees set up since 1948.

The Education Commission (Government of India, 1948) recommended a total switchover from English to Indian languages over a period of time. But only a few years later, the Kunzru Committee (Government of India, 1955) cautioned that a changeover from English to an Indian language as a medium of instruction should not be hastened, and recommended rather vaguely that all university students should continue to 'study' English. The Education Commission (Government of India, 1966), was unusually fairly clear and specific in its assigning definite roles to English, Hindi and the regional languages. It recommended that English be taught and studied as a 'library language' and that Hindi and the regional languages be adopted as mediums of instruction and examination. But the working Group set up by the University Grants Commission (1978) surprisingly enacted a *volte face*, observing that English cannot be dispensed with as a medium of instruction at the level of higher education since the regional languages are not yet developed enough to take over this role.

Recent policy documents on education remain unclear about the medium of instruction. *Challenge of Education* (Government of India, 1985) does not spend much time on the subject, nor does the *National Policy on Education* (1986a) pay much attention to it. *Programme of Action* (1986b), however, does denote a chapter to the question of language development and the medium of instruction. It recommends the adoption of regional languages as mediums of instruction in higher education; it also recommends that facilities for the study of English be augmented and that effective steps be taken to develop Hindi as the link language. But, in spite of these clearly worded recommendations, the reality is that things have not changed at all and the general ambivalence in attitudes and the 'three-medium system' discussed above continue as before.

Thus, as observed above, the three-medium or three-tier system that one can see working in the higher education scenario is a fortuitous development. The water has been allowed to flow on its gravity-driven, seemingly capricious, course. It is now time it was channelled. I would suggest there should be one and the same primary medium of instruction at all levels of education. This could be the relevant regional language. Whatever the criteria for the choice of the medium for a particular region, this medium, once decided upon should be adhered to, but in every region, one or more secondary mediums along with the primary one is essential. This could be Hindi or English or both.

A firm decision on the question of the medium of instruction needs to be taken urgently. One of the reasons why most tertiary campuses are often disturbed is the absence of any such decision. One can see a tug of war going on between the self-styled 'liberal' elitist groups of students and the aggressively defensive firebrand 'nationalists'. This sometimes results in violent agitations and long disruptions of semester or annual schedules, whose causes may be conveniently traced to whatever suits the interests of different social and political groups.

English as a resource language in India

Perhaps the most important, if not the most widespread, use of English is as a library language. This use differs from that in any other country both quantitatively and qualitatively. In respect of quantity, more students and scholars in India use English as a resource language than in any other country in the world, the USA and Britain not excepted. This fact may be attributed to India's enormous population, for even less than 3 per cent of this population, which uses English as a necessary means of communication may outnumber the entire segment of 'educated' population in Great Britain. Regarding quality, the use of English as a resource language in India is utterly incomparable. The overwhelming majority of Indian scholars working on any topic or discipline use reference books in English. Even in Indology, most Indian researchers refer more often to materials in English than in their own regional languages or Hindi. Surprisingly, a sizeable number of them find useful resource materials in English even in respect of purely indigenous subjects – such as Hindi, Tamil or Bangla literature, social reform in India in the nineteenth century, the caste system in India, and so on.

Most encyclopaedias, whatever languages they may have been produced in originally, are available in English. Countless books on the Bible, written anywhere in Christendom or outside it, are accessible in English. Almost all theories of science and knowledge in general that have been propounded, almost all philosophies that have been cerebrated, almost all thoughts that have been conceived since the dawn of civilization are treasured up in English.

If an Indian scholar has no access to any other world language than English, the possibility is that he will not miss out on much. I would say that for India, English is a lifeline for scholarly reference and, seen from this perspective, it is a second language in a special way that is peculiar to India: since all educated people who may ever undertake research of any standard know enough English to utilize references or resources in English, they have a great advantage over many counterparts in the non-English-using world. Thus India, if only by default, occupies a privileged position in its use of English as a resource language, which is the main reason that a number of non-native countries, such as Iran, Iraq, Lybia, Algeria, Nigeria and some Gulf States, notably the People's Democratic Republic of Yemen, employ Indian teachers for the teaching of English.

English as a media language

In the process of enriching the media, English has enriched itself tremendously. The use of English that we find in print journalism today is very different, globally, from any parallel use of English in the first six to seven decades of this century. There is a lot more openness, sometimes even frankness, in the use of vocabulary and more informality in tone and style today. At a reasonably sophisticated level, there is much in common in the use of English in journalism across the globe. In fact, the general global change of attitudes in journalism has both presupposed and entailed a substantial change in the use of English. This change has been given further impetus by demands made on the electronic media. World-wide recreational, informational and instructional expectations have put the already highly expressive mechanisms of English under multifarious pressures, releasing linguistic forms and styles which would have been unthinkable just thirty to forty years ago. Thus, to meet the challenge of the print and the electronic media, English has expanded immensely, both in terms of its coverage and stylistic variation, making it perhaps the most widely used and flexible medium in the world today.

8 Teaching American English as a foreign language: an integrationist approach

DANIEL R. DAVIS

This chapter presents the conception and formulation of a course, 'The Structure of American English', taught at the English Department at the University of Hong Kong and discusses why and how an integrationist approach to the study of American English can illuminate students' experience of language in the political and sociocultural context of Hong Kong. The relevance of this chapter extends to the teaching of linguistics and varieties of English in both first and second language situations, and the thesis can be summarized as follows: Linguistics and 'standard languages' should not be taught as a set of techniques of analysis and objects for analysis. Instead, they should be taught as a set of cultural, intellectual practices arising in a particular historical, cultural, intellectual, and above all, political context. By making this (sometimes difficult and frustrating) shift, language and linguistics teachers can empower their students, first, by de-reifying and de-mystifying language and linguistics, second, by situating linguistics within various political and intellectual discourses, recognizing linguists as responsive actors within these discourses, and finally, by making students aware of the political and social consequences of their own acts as linguists.

'English, Whose English?' (the title of the conference for which this chapter was written as a paper) is a controversial question in at least two ways. First, because it is a loaded question, demanding an answer which stakes a claim on the language. Second, because it makes the theoretical assumption that 'English' (whatever it may be) is the sort of entity which can be possessed. The question thus begs another: 'English, What's English?'

The integrationist critique of linguistics begins with a similar question, 'What is a language?', as posed by linguistic theorists (see Harris, 1980).

Linguistic theorists advance this question not in a genuine spirit of inquiry, but as a rhetorical ploy to introduce their own definitions of a language. Integrationism sees language (and linguistics, being a kind of language) strictly as an integral aspect of human behaviour, and therefore gives priority to identifying the intellectual and cultural contexts of various answers (explicit or assumed, sincere or otherwise) to the question, 'What is a language?' For an integrational linguistics, the definition of language and *a* language is fluid and dependent on context; the integrationist enterprise is essentially to identify and re-identify the contexts significant to linguistic and metalinguistic behaviour.

My purpose here is not to define the terms 'English' or 'a language', but to identify this as the centre of the discussion. In the case of the specific example presented by this chapter, I wish to start the discussion by opening up the definition of 'American English' and leaving it open, turning instead to the contexts which bear on this definition.

The first context to be addressed is that of the students of the course, with particular reference to the language in the University of Hong Kong and in Hong Kong in general. Students arrive at the Arts Faculty at the University from a society which is multilingual, with languages such as Cantonese, English, Putonghua, Chiu Chow, Hakka, Shanghainese, Tagalog, Portuguese, Hindi spoken by different groups within the community. There is a high degree of variation within the English spoken in Hong Kong, owing to its second-language status for most of the community, and to the widespread geographical origin of first-language speakers. At the same time, there is widespread awareness of the political and economic significance of language in general and English in particular. This has to do with the role of English within the colonial history of Hong Kong, but also with the rapid modernization and development of the Hong Kong economy since the Second World War, and concerns for the future of Hong Kong in post-1997 Asia. Perceptions of English are arguably quite complex: it is seen as essential to the economic success of Hong Kong within the Pacific; it is part of the modern cosmopolitan identity of Hong Kong; but it can also be perceived as the heritage of colonial and imperialist rule. There is a considerable amount of insecurity about language in Hong Kong, especially among that part of the population attending university. This is witnessed in the perennial debate about language *standards* in education, seen in the *South China Morning Post* and the *Hong Kong Standard* newspapers, and in the question asked of academics, 'What do you think of the students' standard of English?'

It is within this linguistic and social situation that the course, 'The Structure of American English', has been offered for two years in the Arts Faculty at the University of Hong Kong, where it has been very popular. The students' reasons for taking the course fall into two groups: the first centres on the perceived utility of American English for doing business with Americans in Hong Kong; the second may be that students have various contacts with North America such as the emigration of relatives and the import of American popular culture to Hong Kong. When asked, students tend to refer to the former reason (the economic importance), or to express an interest in learning *the features of American English*.

There are a number of ways to design a course on this subject for an audience with these expectations, in this linguistic situation, each with its own drawbacks. One could give a structural account, identifying the features of American English. This has the advantage of meeting the students' expectations, and there are very useful texts such as Trudgill and Hannah (1982) which are readily available. However, this strategy becomes in practice a comparison with other varieties rather than a true structuralist description of 'the American Language'. More importantly, this strategy plays into some of the language myths which already beset the students, the myth of a standard language especially. On the one hand, the students have a large investment in the concept of a standard language, since their success in examinations has placed them at the top of the educational ladder in Hong Kong, and this will determine their place in society. On the other hand, acceptance of the mantle of the standard language places them in a permanent crisis of identity. Is their English of a sufficient standard? Is it necessary to defer to speakers of English as a first language? Does conformity to a standard result in a transferral of loyalty from Hong Kong or China to some other place, especially if it results in a usage noticeably different from that of their peers? A structuralist approach gives them a method for learning a variety of English, feature by feature, but in doing so it denies them the possibility of addressing the political situation it has landed them in.

A different way to structure the course would be to give a socio-historical account of the development of American English, explaining the diachronic development of various features of American English in society (usually relating specific features to historical events or social trends or processes). Again, there are easily obtainable books such as Marckwardt (1980), McCrum *et al.* (1986) and Dillard (1992). Unfortunately (and perhaps surprisingly), such an approach meets neither the students' expectations nor their interests. They do not see the relevance of such an approach, and I would advance the explanation that the social history of American English assumes a set of values embodied in the American experience to which they have little if any access and to which they find it difficult to relate. Furthermore, because they rarely have a background in American history, this approach tends to become a history lesson rather than a study of language.

The important point about both of these strategies is that the role they expect of the teacher is as an insider, an American, initiating the students as outsiders into the rules and values of the entity 'American English'. This is perhaps a role which the TEFL teacher is required to play at times, but in this context the role is not appropriate, for the following reasons. First, the students have relatively fluent English. Second, the initiation is not part of a training in linguistics at the University level. Finally, and more importantly, it is not acceptable ideologically, in that it propagates myths of language which deny the students possession of the language. It assumes that language is inherently and entirely national in its constitution, and in doing this ignores the issues of identity (both political and cultural) bound up in language. The initiation relies on linguistic and cultural stereotyping without recognizing that it does so.

It is for these reasons that I decided not to adopt either of these strategies as a framework for the course, but to formulate an integrationist strategy. As I have said above, such an approach must begin with contexts, and the discussion up to now can be said to embody three positions or contexts: the students', my own as teacher, and that of the subject matter. The students, for the reasons mentioned earlier, are interested in features of American English. My own position (as a teacher of university undergraduates and as a linguist) is to encourage reasoned and critical thought, writing and discussion in the students, centring on the subject and its definition. The subject, for its part, presents a number of possible approaches to students, which are to be found in its literature and which can (and should) be incorporated into an overall integrational approach. This should identify the concerns and intellectual and political context of each text. Criticism of the texts in which these various approaches are found is the proper beginning of an integrational discussion. But for the purposes of integrational teaching, the students' expectation must first be addressed. This amounts to a simultaneous introduction to and attack on the notion of linguistic features.

The text used as the object of criticism for this is Trudgill and Hannah (1982), *International English*. This book presents so-called standard varieties of English by means of lists of phonological, grammatical, lexical and orthographical features. The text is valuable in that it is simple enough for the students to digest quickly, but it is sufficiently detailed to capture some of the complexities and contradictions involved in setting up standard varieties. Its use of minimal pairs and the notion of phonemes to set up a sound system for each variety points up its debt to structuralist discovery methods, and ultimately to structuralism itself. By setting the linguistic feature within this intellectual tradition, it can be shown that, at least within structuralist theory and methodology, the linguistic feature has no existence apart from the network of relations in which it is embedded, and in fact, can be said to be constituted by the system as a whole. Since pure Saussurean structuralism does not allow direct mapping between features in different systems, the theoretical problem for varieties of English is that either each variety is a system in its own right, in which case its features cannot be compared to those of another variety, or, each variety is seen to exist within one system, in which case it is to be banished to the realm of *parole* as the idiosyncrasies of an individual or group of individuals within the community. Nor can the use of the term 'national standard language' remove this theoretical problem, since what makes one dialect the standard is not part of synchronic linguistics as defined by Saussure.

There is no linguistic reason to equate the standard language with the linguistic system.

Linguistic features which derive from structuralist method are thereby shown to pose problems for the linguist trying to use them to define different varieties of English. The next part of the attack on linguistic features in the course involves the examination of texts in order to identify varieties of English within them. As an exercise, this requires students to apply their reading of *International English* and its features to selected texts from various origins, trying to state the origin of text on the basis of linguistic features. This exercise achieves a number of tasks. First, it satisfies the students' curiosity about linguistic features, and points up how difficult such identification of variety on the basis of features is. Second, it shows that so-called 'American English' features exist outside of 'American English', and that 'non-American English' features exist within 'American English'. That is, not only are there theoretical difficulties with the notion 'linguistic feature', but there are also serious difficulties in applying the notion to linguistic behaviour, even if a 'practical' or non-theoretical stance is taken regarding the existence of linguistic features. Distinctions such as standard/non-standard are shown to be just as useful (that is, of very limited usefulness) as the American/British or American/non-American distinction in accounting for the language of a text. The exercise usually reveals certain stereotypes which the students have formed about American English, the crudest being that all non-standard English is American English (for example, that the form 'ain't' and the double negative are exclusive to American English). This hypothesis can be easily shown to be a stereotype by including an English dialect text. But the point is not to ensure that the students' stereotypes of or hypotheses about American English converge with those in Trudgill and Hannah; rather it is to show that all hypotheses about linguistic features and varieties involve stereotyping. Variation within and across national borders can be used to show that all national varieties are political constructs based on the stereotyping of features. It is undeniable that in a dialect continuum some isoglosses for certain features may be shown to run along a national boundary; but the perception that these are the significant aspects of variation upon which to concentrate is ultimately determined by political orientation. This raises difficult problems about the political implications of standard language varieties (and in fact, the entire method of using varieties as a means of rationalizing linguistic variation) for individual identity. A final point brought up by the exercise is that authors (and speakers) can of course manipulate features (as they perceive them) to achieve various ends.

The result of this two-pronged introduction and attack on features is, it is to be hoped, that the students learn both features (as they desired originally) and, more importantly, their theoretical and practical limitations. Also, it should be noted that an attempt is made to address their possible experience of American English in Hong Kong, first through literature, and second through their everyday life. They are asked, as another assignment, to make a phonetic transcription of a news broadcast and to say whether the news reader is British, American, Canadian, or a speaker of some other variety. This is not to be interpreted as an attempt to make latter-day Professor Higginses of them, but to illustrate by direct appeal to their (almost) everyday experience, the fact that judgements are made on the basis of perceived accent, and that these judgements often have political and social significance, particularly if the newsreader is from Hong Kong but has lived overseas in Britain, Canada, the United States, Australia. (As an aside, it should be mentioned that many of the students arrive at university unable to distinguish between American, British, Canadian and Australian accents, perceiving them all as 'foreign'. I am indebted to K. Bolton for suggesting and corroborating this observation.)

The course then turns to other approaches to American English as manifest in a variety of texts. The texts are used to situate the study of American English within various political and intellectual discourses. The texts are Marckwardt (1980) (an example of what I call the 'social historical' approach), Hans Kurath (1972) (the 'dialectological' approach), William Labov (1972) (the 'sociolinguistic' approach), J. Dillard (1972) (the issue of Black English), and Noah Webster (in Crowley, 1991) (the 'political' approach). Each passage has been selected because it exemplifies or characterizes a set of assumptions about language and because it addresses certain arguments, often unstated, within the study of American English. The students are asked to work out what the linguistic assumptions are within each text, and to consider these assumptions in the light of the argument of each text. The aim of the exercise is first, to give them some familiarity with linguistic issues in the study of American English and second, to illustrate the Saussurean structuralist principle that, where language is concerned, the point of view creates the object of study.

The passage from Marckwardt is taken from the chapter entitled 'Colonial Lag and Levelling'. In it the assumption is made that there is a direct correlation between linguistic change or stability (and the resulting features of a variety) and specific aspects of social change and stability. This is not too controversial (although it is not strictly structuralist), nor does it produce too striking a view of language, but it clearly plays into an argument about the authenticity and 'originality' of American English vis-à-vis British English. For Marckwardt, American English is linguistically conservative just as American society is socially conservative; when there are instances of clear innovation on the part of American English, Marckwardt takes great pains to situate this within sixteenth- to eighteenth-century development in British English. Since he has earlier argued that the language of the first colonists is the language of Shakespeare and Marlowe, one can easily make out that his argument is concerned with validating American English as closer to the language of the cultural icons of the English speaking world. This is in answer to a criticism (unstated in this text) of the innovative, 'nouveau', uncultured aspect of American English (and the influence it has had on other varieties of English in the twentieth century).

This sort of re-situation and recovery of American English within the English cultural world has its linguistic counterpart in Kurath's article. His ostensible problem is to explain the relation between American English dialects and British English dialects, but the article can also be read as an answer to the question, 'How many structural linguistic systems exist within the Anglo-American English-speaking community/ies, one or two?'

The difficulty with the overt problem is that some of the same variation occurring within British English dialects occurs within American English dialects (though the dialects themselves cannot be said to have been transplanted), yet, structurally speaking, American English observes for the most part the same mergers and splits that 'Standard British English' (to use Kurath's term) does. Kurath's solution is to argue that British English and American share the same set of phonemes, although these are in different lexical distribution in the two varieties. Regional variation is said to be sub-phonemic. What is interesting about this claim is that it argues that there is one sound system of English, equivalent to the standard, and that there is in fact one English language. This is the only position which a structuralist could afford to take in dealing with variation, as any admission of variation within the system proper would allow the possibility not only of two systems, American and British, but of any number of systems based on different dialects, with the result that the English language would disintegrate into a very large number of separate systems, or that it would consist of one system with so much internal variation as to bring into question its status as a system in any sense. Kurath's point of view has created the English language as he sees it.

Issues of language definition and status also arise in 'The Social Motivation of a Sound Change'. In this article Labov (or at least, the early Labov) attempts to explain linguistic change in its social setting. In the particular case of centralized diphthongs in Martha's Vineyard, Labov relates a high frequency of centralized diphthongs to a political orientation towards the island and its values, in opposition to those of the mainland. However, despite recognizing the social and political setting of variation and change, Labov denies the claim by one of the islanders that the language of Martha's Vineyard is a different variety, a 'separate language within the English language' (Labov, 1972: 29). For him, the definition of language and variety is still an issue of structural facts, not a question of political interpretation, and it is the province of the trained linguist. I find it instructive to point out to students that, on the basis of linguistic features, the language Labov describes in Martha's Vineyard is as different from the 'US English' described by Trudgill and Hannah as their 'Canadian English' is.

The definition of a language or variety is dealt with in 'Black English and the Academic Establishment', in Dillard (1972). Dillard makes the case that in earlier discussions of the English of Blacks in the United States, linguists were misled by their political prejudices in saying that a distinct variety, 'Black English', did not exist. He goes on to discuss the political and educational implications of the status of Black English as dialect or variety. Clearly, it is of extreme importance for him to argue that Black English is a separate variety of English, both in terms of its structure and its historical origin, and that this distinct status merits special educational treatment for the speakers of this variety. From this chapter it can be seen that the political point of view as much as the linguistic point of view creates the object of study (and its history), and further, that a linguist is to be held responsible for both his politics and the political implications of the analysis of language which he puts forward.

The final text used in the course is Noah Webster's essay on reforming spelling, 'An Essay on the Necessity, Advantages and Practicability of Reforming the Mode of Spelling, and of Rendering the Orthography of Words Consistent to the Pronunciation' (Appendix to *Dissertations on the English Language*, 1789, reprinted in Crowley, 1991). Webster's approach to language can be said to be political: it is clear from his discussion and examples that he assumes language to be a political and social institution. He makes the specific point that the distinction between American and British English can be reinforced by changing the spelling system (which for Webster is part of the language), and that this change would result in pride in American literature, language, and culture in opposition to (and freed from dependence on) British literature, language, and culture. For Webster, political reality is at least in part based on language, and a linguist is one who can change language to reinforce a political reality. Alone among all the other linguists dealt with in this chapter and course, he recognizes both the responsibility and the power of the linguist. He alone recognizes his role as actor within a political and linguistic discourse; he alone illustrates (and indeed requires) that the relation between point of view and language is reciprocal: the point of view creates the object of study creates the point of view . . .

One might ask, how is this course 'integrational'? First, it de-segregates language, in the first place by calling into question segregationist linguistic categories and a segregationist system of language (i.e. the structuralist position), and in the second by re-siting language ('American English') within the students' experience of English in Hong Kong. Second, the course studies the *metalinguistic* behaviour which constitutes and defines the terms 'American', 'English', and 'American English'. Third, it considers the responsibility and power of linguists as political agents within an intellectual, social, cultural and political situation, and finally, it extends this role to students.

One can consider this form of empowerment in terms of cost and benefit. The first cost is that the notion of 'standard' English is lost; the benefit is that students may realize the contingency of this notion according to various purposes within a political situation. This could be of considerable value in Hong Kong society.

Second, the status of the linguist as trained expert putting forward description and analysis of language, is put in question. Against this cost, one may place the benefit that by abandoning aspirations to this status, students may realize their own political power and responsibility as linguists. Also, as a return for weakening the notion of systematicity, one may find that the Saussurean principle of point of view is perhaps a better position from which to appreciate the nature of human language.

Third, the credibility of stereotypical national identities formed on the basis of stereotyped linguistic features has been brought down. They are of course still in existence and available as screens to hide behind for the individual who so chooses. But they are no longer shelter, only cover. To leave these stereotypes is to heighten one's sensibility to issues of language and identity: different political manifestations of the individual are made possible.

Finally, the course clearly limits the power of analytical methodology in linguistics. On the credit side, it develops one's critical faculty towards linguistic theory and language studies.

During the last tutorial of the course, I usually ask students to consider what significance these issues in the study of American English may have for the linguistics of English in Hong Kong. So far, reactions vary, with some quite enthusiastic, others perceptive and cautious, and others uninspired and unresponsive. It is perhaps too easy to make facile comparisons which may obscure rather than illuminate their linguistic and political experience. At any rate, my aim is not to expose them to a political ideology, but to an ideology about the political role of the linguist. It is their decision whether to adopt this role, or to turn to other forms of linguistics, and the roles they provide.

Acknowledgements

I would like to thank Professor R. Harris, Mr K. Bolton, and Dr C. Hutton for reading this paper and commenting upon it.

9 Owning English in teacher education

DIANNE SIRNA MANCUS

Herbert Kohl (1992) in an article titled 'I Won't Learn From You/Thoughts on the Role of Assent in Learning' discusses the phenomenon of wilful not-learning, often mis-labelled by teachers as failure. Capable people, he argues sometimes make conscious decisions not to learn from teachers they feel they cannot trust. He says that in these cases, because the students have never tried, they should not be diagnosed as having failed: refusal to learn is a rational response to a perceived personal or cultural threat. Kohl illustrates this point by describing the grandfather of one of his Hispanic students who refused to learn English. The grandfather said that he was afraid his grandchildren would not learn Spanish if everyone spoke with them in English, and that their culture would not survive if the language was lost: people might be destroyed by learning what others wanted them to learn.

Kohl (1992) describes refusal to learn as a way of protecting culture, integrity, and identity, adding that students exchange failing grades to protect their personal and cultural integrity. He insists that teachers and school systems must be able to discriminate between failure to learn and wilful not-learning. Kohl's solution for wilful not-learning are teachers who are committed to political activism for social justice. When teachers share this commitment with students, a basis of trust is established and learning can take place.

In Jonathan Kozol's *Illiterate America* (1985) the failure of American schools is well documented, placing the number of functionally illiterate adults in the United States at 60 million. He criticizes low-level literacy training in the US Army and extols the use of people's own stories of struggle as the text for community-based adult literacy instruction. Kozol includes application, compassion, and ethical decision making as important dimensions of modern literacy. Like Paulo Freire, Michael Apple and Henry Giroux, Kozol claims that curricular decisions are always political. What is taught? Who is taught, for what purpose, by whom, and in what manner?

Although school districts in low-income communities of the United States continually look for *fool-proof* methods which will affect performance and validate that learning has taken place by improved test scores, I will argue in this chapter that it is essential to address the personal, cultural, and political implications of literacy learning if many students are to learn in school at all. An unasked but critical question should be: how does the method used for literacy enhancement affect power relationships and student–teacher trust? Do students see the method as helping them meet their own purposes or in their perception does the pedagogy ask them to function outside or in opposition to that which is important to them? Ultimately, the question comes down to 'How will the method influence the students' willingness to become engaged in learning?' The role of assent in learning and the political nature of pedagogy must be considered when we seek solutions to illiteracy, under-achievement, and the escalating school drop-out rate, particularly for minorities.

Teacher education students who have experienced first-hand the social stigmatization attached to non-English or non-standard dialect speakers readily understand the politics of language and language study. I have worked with Appalachian Mountain people, West Indian students in the Virgin Islands, African American students from urban areas of the US, and Hispanic students in New Mexico, and they quickly get the point, i.e. language is a highly political instrument used by the establishment to assess intelligence and for the assignment of social and economic class. Furthermore, they understand the role the school plays in this categorization and labelling of low-income, working class and minority peoples.

I have found, however, that the political nature of language and of curricular decisions for teaching literacy are not so readily understood by those who speak *television talk* and live within 'mainstream' culture, the particular group which supplies most US teachers. What I have found as a helpful corollary to teaching classroom practices for empowerment through literacy is to consider the nature of language as revealed in the social and political history of various languages. By examining language-related issues of class, culture, and domination now and in other times and places, teacher education students are better able to understand the potential for political and personal conflict which language and literacy learning creates for all those except white, middle-class Americans from the Midwest. What emerges when the study of language pedagogy is tied to philosophy, history and politics, is a personal discovery, a reconstruction, by the prospective teacher of the nature of language and of important principles for working effectively and respectfully with diverse populations.

The examination of particular social/historical situations can help in the discovery of important principles about language and help in the design and selection of critical pedagogy for literacy enhancement. I will illustrate how this knowledge influenced the work of teacher education students in a literacy project with racially diverse children from low-income families.

(1) Language changes over time and across situations.
Within the first two to three weeks of the class, students read a brief history of the English language. As they come to understand how English has changed

over the years due to various invaders and visitors to England (the Vikings, the Danes, the French, and so on) the transplanting of English to other countries, and changing needs of the people (invention of the printing press, increased leisure time for reading, new technology, and so on), they come to see language as a dynamic medium which belongs to people and is subject to their management and creativity. This knowledge is essential later in the course when a case is made that no truly standard language exists, because language is subject to moulding by the speaker, the listener, the context and the purpose for speaking. Knowledge that language conventions emerged to aid primarily written communication, after the invention of the printing press, makes written language conventions seem less like royal guardians of one linguistic ideal, and more like a servant of the speaker, reader or writer.

(2a) Non-standard dialects develop due to geographical barriers and cultural distinctions.
(2b) Dialect is a complete language system quite satisfactory for communication within the community of its speakers.
An analysis of British-sounding English still spoken today along the Chesapeake Bay on the East Coast of the United States and of dialects spoken in isolated regions of the Appalachian Mountains or the Georgia Sea Islands, helps students to understand that common culture and geographical isolation over time result in vocabulary or pronunciation specific to a particular region or people. Students then recognize that language differences emerge due to particular communication needs and common experiences. Hopefully, they discover that dialect is a complete language system, fully appropriate for use in its place and time by native speakers who know and understand its nuances.

(3a) Culture, community, identity and belonging are bound up in the speech of our families, our mother tongues.
(3b) We may choose to add the dialect or language of the dominant class to our linguistic repertoire in order to carry out successful transactions with the dominant culture and thereby protect our own culture and community.
As students examine the development of dialects in particular regions by particular peoples, they come to see that language is an essential part of culture. On a recent trip to Guatemala to learn Spanish, I learned that there are twenty-two different tribes of Mayan peoples of Guatemala. Not only do these tribes have distinctive clothing with colours and symbols which identify them with their community, they speak unique Mayan dialects and carry on ancient rituals and art forms which aid them in recognizing one another and in keeping secrets from those who would destroy their culture. Ancient dialects help the people preserve their ancestral ways and maintain cultural cohesion.

Members of the controlling minority in Guatemala, the government, military, and *ladino* (mixed Spanish and Indian) shopkeepers as well as some of the *ladino* poor, resent the traditional adherence of indigenous peoples to old customs and ancient languages. But their adherence to traditional practices has been an essential agent in the amazing ability of the Mayan peoples of Guatemala to survive five hundred years of colonization and to actively resist what has been called the greatest human rights violations in the world. On the other hand, Rigoberta Menchu, a Guatemalan Indian woman who was recently presented the Nobel Peace Prize, said that she decided to learn Spanish for self-protection and cultural preservation. She did not want to have others continue to speak for Indians (Menchu, 1984: 156). Menchu learned Spanish because she wanted to tell the world about the five hundred year oppression of her people and of their courageous resistance (p. xii).

(4a) The designations 'lower class' and 'upper class' speech are often arbitrary and not based on any defensible criteria.
From 1960–64, John F. Kennedy of Boston, Massachusetts, served as the President of the United States. New Englanders are known for their own particular dialect, but unlike the southern or Appalachian dialects in the United States, this one is considered 'posh' and educated. During the Cuban Missile Crisis, Kennedy would speak of 'Cuber' for Cuba. It was considered acceptable and quaint when Kennedy pronounced the last syllable as /er/. However, when Appalachian people and rural Southerners say 'winder' for window, it is not considered quaint but *hickish,* as Leon Williamson (1978), a college professor who grew up in a poor sharecropper family in Florida, wrote in his poem 'To Climb Their Success Ladder', which is used in the class.

(4b) The status of a people determines the status of their language.
In our examination of the history of the English language, we linger at the period of the Norman Conquest. It is important for students to realize that English has not always been the premier language of the world. When the Norman nobles moved to England following the victory of their leader William the Conqueror, English as the language of the working-class people was considered less desirable and French became the language of nobility. It is interesting to note that, nevertheless, English women and men chose to continue to speak their language as a matter of patriotism, cultural identity and resistance.

The relationship of economics to linguistic and cultural status is understood in an examination of this period. The result of the shortage of labour which followed the Black Death, the decline of feudalism, and the emergence of craftsmen and a middle class, was a blending of the two languages. English people learned French to assist in upward mobility, but also maintained their use of English as a form of cultural identity. The French noble class learned English in order to converse with labourers and get the services they wanted. At this time, there were major changes to the English language in intonation, vocabulary, and the dropping of inflectional endings, resulting from the influence of French on English. It is also interesting to point out that while

French was the language of the elite in Britain, the French dialect spoken in the British Isles was considered inferior to French as it was spoken on the continent.

Conflicts during this period and those today over use of Spanish in urban areas like Miami and Los Angeles are clearly parallel. It is at this point in the class that we study law-makers' ambivalence towards bilingual education as played out in periodic re-authorizations of the US Bilingual Education Act and the motivation of those working for passage of an 'English-only' amendment to the US Constitution.

(5a) The educational system, as the transmitter of the dominant culture's values, discriminates for cultural, not educational reasons against students who speak 'non-standard' dialects or languages other than the dominant one, English.

(5b) The school system could facilitate literacy acquisition and standard language learning by encouraging bi-dialectalism and/or bi-lingualism.

Students are now ready to assess the role of the school in carrying out class oppression and to tackle the design of pedagogy which uses native language or dialect as a bridge to second language or conventional dialect learning. They have come to understand that when use of one's native language or dialect is denigrated and/or forbidden, students are likely to become silent, insecure, anxious, resistant, and less able to tackle new language learning.

An important tool of colonization and oppression has been to convince the conquered that they are indeed inferior. This is accomplished, in part, by not allowing disenfranchised peoples to learn the language of the powerful and then ridiculing their informal attempts to do so. Pidgin English, now recognized as an official language in New Melanesia, and various English-speaking Creoles are examples of the creative efforts of conquered peoples to learn the language of the conqueror. Today in the Southwestern United States, teachers, business people, and politicians speak derisively of *Spanglesh* or *Texacan* and argue that *Latino* children are not conversant in English or Spanish. It is well to remember, however, that dialect speakers are able to understand *standard* speech. It is the speaker of *standard* language who cannot understand dialect. If we are not satisfied with Creole languages, then we must offer strong bilingual education programmes.

Political oppression of Native Peoples in North America has been carried out through linguistic control and the requirement of total assimilation. Although the Cherokees, Creeks, Choctaws, and Seminoles had their own schools using their own languages, the expansionist United States government eventually took Native American children to residential schools far from home where they were not permitted to wear traditional clothes or speak their native languages. A government report of 1868, motivated by a combination of humanitarianism, militarism and expansionism, blamed difference in language as the source of problems with the Indians and recommended the establishment of schools to blot out 'barbarous dialects' (in Leibowitz, 1978: 6).

(6) Pedagogy is never neutral. Who *teaches* what *to* whom? Why? *and* How? *are questions of great importance.*

An integral part of the course is The Write Partnership in which university interns spend one-half day in an elementary school serving low-income and racially and culturally diverse students. They work in whole language activities with one or two first graders (6–7 year-olds) and in a writing workshop with two fifth graders (10–11 year-olds). They also spend two to three hours per week on campus in the university course described above. The field experience begins with shared fruit and conversation and moves on to shared stories. On the first day, both interns and children make 'an important person tree' and get better acquainted by talking about their family members and friends. Names of special people are the first words to go in a word bank kept during the semester.

Each week, first graders are encouraged to draw and write their own stories about a friend or family member. As a result, words of great meaning are added to their word banks each week. Invented spellings are celebrated and, although there is a lot of talk exchanged about the stories, interns encourage students to be as independent as they can be in putting words on paper. Students write in the natural cadence of their home language. Fifth graders begin to formalize their language as they write for more distant audiences, for example, a published book of animal stories.

Oftentimes, students write about their teacher, Mrs Pederson. One Chinese American child wrote, 'Mrs Pederson has a lot of money.' When his teacher asked him why he wrote that, he said, 'because you are always buying things for us.' As a result of our work with two Chinese twins who consistently wrote 'I have, he have, you have, John have,' and so on, the classroom teacher learned from one of the university interns that there is no singular or plural verb form in Chinese. A home visit was planned which included the university intern, the classroom teacher, and a Chinese-American university professor. During this visit the teacher also learned that the orientation of Chinese print is not left to right, a very important piece of information for a first grade teacher of Chinese children.

Children in the project write about their parent's pregnancies, weddings, skirmishes with the law and other situations which sometimes surprise their privileged university student interns. One Mexican-American girl wrote, 'My mother helps Chicanos.' The classroom teacher asked us to translate all Spanish words used in the writing, including Chicano, which is really a term used in the United States to describe Mexican-Americans.

First graders write one hard-bound, laminated book each week. These books are kept in their class library and children enjoy reading each other's books throughout the term. The classroom teacher often extends the book writing activity during the week, using the children's work in other activities. University interns always bring a magic bag full of picture books from which children choose one to be read aloud. First graders write poems about colours, wishes, dreams, and lies, and they dramatize one of their favourite books.

Very early in the term, university students bring a rough draft of a biographical piece they have written to the fifth graders and ask for help revising it for a fifth grade audience. At first children are reluctant to make any suggestions or ask for additional information; they are afraid of hurting their new teacher's feelings by being critical in any way. The university professor also brings drafts of stories about her own childhood in West Virginia, and the boys and girls help her revise the work. They have helped her revise stories and poems about her mother's favourite dog which chased cars and was poisoned by a neighbour and about the time she and her brother set the neighbour's field on fire while making toast bread. This use of the writing conference for revision makes a profound impression on the children and the interns' understanding of what collaboration can do to make a piece of writing better. Reluctance both to criticize others and to revise one's own work diminishes as the writing partners focus on the story, its audience, and making the story better. Fifth graders and university interns also spend some of every period writing in their own journals and sharing those entries with one another when they choose to do so. Each child and each university intern assist one another in revising at least one autobiographical piece to be made into a cloth-bound book. They also write poetry and read stories together. The final project with the older children is collaborative research and writing about a favourite animal. The animal piece may be fictional but based on actual facts about the animal, or it may be strictly expository. The children write, revise and edit in pairs with the help of their university teacher. Their final work is published in a class book and duplicated for each writer.

Just as children write about births, they also write poignant stories about the death of loved ones. One first grader wrote about a fire in a mobile home in which her grandmother and cousin had died the weekend before. A fifth grader wrote about the gunshot death of her 13-year-old cousin, Pamela Jean.

> It happened a long time ago when I was in third grade. I was sad and when she died her funeral was on Easter night and I had nightmares about her and still now I have nightmares about her.
>
> When I hear this song called, *Since I Lost My Baby* by Luther Vandross, I think about what she would be like driving in a car and what kind of car it would be and how tall she would be at age sixteen.
>
> (Johnson, 1992)

Another child and her partner worked hard on a story about the mixture of pain and satisfaction of moving away 'from this place' where 'there are too many gang fights and drug dealers' and where 'nobody will rent to my mom because she's got four kids'. One child told about being arrested for shoplifting when his cousin was the real culprit. In an expository piece about wild cats, one fifth grader wrote, 'My two uncles hunt wild cats all over North America.'

The children's stories and poetry give support to Herbert's (1974) contention that children have enough real-life experiences to fill their own history books. McGinley and Kamberelis (1992) found that when children wrote about their own lives and experiences they came to understand writing as a social and political activity. Asante *et al.* (1991) reported that children are more interested in school and focused on their work when their own culture is the centre of the curriculum. We certainly have found this to be true in The Write Partnership. An added advantage of our autobiographical writing is that pre-service teacher education students learn a lot about children whose homes, families, cultures, languages and dialects may be very different from their own. As a result of shared stories, our interns come to know in an existential way the value of the child's text as the medium for literacy acquisition.

During the last meeting of the term, children and parents come to campus for personalized guided tours of dormitory rooms, the interactive video centre, swimming pool, snack bar, library and classrooms. University students take their guests to all of their favourite and familiar campus places. We initiated the visit to campus when one fifth grade child asked an intern if she rode a bus to school. When the intern informed the child that she lived at school, the child asked, 'Do you sleep in the classroom?'

The field trip is followed by a Young Author's Reception, where individual certificates for published books are presented to the children by the interns. The president of the university reads some of their work, congratulates the children, and speaks to them about the fun and importance of writing. It is often a tearful goodbye as the children get on their bus and return to school. In their thank-you letters, they write about 'My College.' This is just how we want them to think about the university. We want them to see themselves as writers with important ideas to communicate, as readers with valuable purposes for reading, and we want them to picture themselves, at a very young age, as students on a university campus some day.

University students leave the course with philosophical, historical, and linguistic knowledge, as well as practical wisdom from classroom experience. This will serve them well as they make instructional decisions for children from diverse backgrounds, with different languages and dialects. It will no doubt help them to argue more reasonably and convincingly as classroom teachers with those who wish to mould children by establishing narrow educational goals through a national curriculum.

10 Reclaiming the canon: the case for adolescent literature

MARY LOFTIN GRIMES AND
SUZANNE BARTON BELOTE

Recent attacks in both England and America on 'non-canonical' literature reflect efforts to standardize the curriculum and to limit classroom teachers' presentation of selections other than those considered classics, that is works produced by Anglo-Saxon writers, mostly male, prior to the Second World War. The result of such trends is to deny the experience and values of increasing numbers of students, making this group's education less relevant than it should be. Perhaps one would do well to consider, as a starting point for addressing this issue, the purposes for which literature is taught in secondary schools.

Foremost among such purposes is the desire to instil appreciation of literature, with students developing the habit of reading for pleasure. Closely allied is the assumption that, through literary experiences, students will gain an understanding of humanity which will help them deal more effectively with people in real-life situations. In addition, it is via literature study that teachers familiarize students with literary conventions which, in turn, contribute to their ability to understand that medium. Literature study also allows students to experience vicariously many situations common among their peers. Further, it serves as a model for student writers to emulate. And, according to William Bennett, literature '[shapes] sensibility, [develops] good habits of character, and [lifts] the imagination beyond the limits of a too narrowly imposed boundary of self-definition' (cited in O'Donnell, 1984: 86).

Official decision makers, such as developers of state/national curricular guidelines, add to the above list the following assumptions regarding the function of literature in the curriculum: it is there to transmit the canon of recognized masterpieces, and it should prepare students for further study, which requires passing tests of some sort. In fact, politicians frequently appear not to recognize goals other than these last two, and disparage practitioners' attempts to present literature to students in ways which are personally, socially, or cultur-ally meaningful. Recent attacks in both England and America on 'non-canonical' literature reflect a growing conservative influence over curricular decisions, particularly with regard to titles appropriate for study. And while not all works identified as suspect would be perceived as extra-canonical, many do belong to the adolescent literature genre. The National Council of Teachers of English (Davis, 1992) reports challenges, for example, to the following texts, among others, during 1992: *Bridge to Terabithia* by Katherine Paterson (1977), *Grendel* by John Gardner (1972), *Blubber* by Judy Blume (1974), *I Am the Cheese* by Robert Cormier (1977), and *The Boy Who Drank Too Much* by Shep Greene (1979). Typically, these texts were objected to for containing one or more of what the Council calls 'the three S's—sex, swear words, and Satanism', but some were also cited for containing 'less than uplifting situations' (Davis, 1992: 13). Several familiar titles often classified as adolescent literature have a long and distinguished history of reappearance on this list: the most frequently challenged authors include J. D. Salinger, Mark Twain, Madeline L'Engle, John Steinbeck, Shel Silverstein, as well as Blume and Cormier.

The increased tendency towards centralized control, such as that residing in Great Britain's 1988 Education Reform Act, invariably affords increased potential for uninformed decision making, which, however well-intended, can frustrate its own aims. Such decisions, frequently executed under the aegis of economy or even patriotism (recall the McCarthy Hearings) often result in accomplishing neither of these intents. This might be less alarming if societies were homogeneous. But the current conservative bias among external shapers of curriculum fails to address the needs of a growing body of students for whom the classics, as defined by those in power, have little connection with their personal, social, or cultural reality. Assumptions about minority/immi-grant students, for example, frequently ignore the need to bridge cultures, and so fail to engage many of those students. Typically these groups are expected to assimilate with the dominant culture with relatively little assistance. Yet for many this acculturation does not occur, with the result that minority/immigrant populations 'tend not to succeed in school and out, and . . . to assume subordinate roles in society' (Grant and Sleeter, 1988: 19) Words like 'rigour', 'tradition', and 'value for money' may sound appealing to political constituents, but hardly translate, for increasingly large numbers of students, to a concern for those students' 'spiritual, moral, cultural, mental, and physical development' nor do they prepare them for 'the opportunities, responsibilities, and experiences of adult life' (*Education Reform Act*, cited in Martin Leonard, 1988: 3).

We need not look far for evidence that students are being imperfectly prepared for adult life. While high levels of unemployment reflect causes in addition to under-preparation, the instances of sociopathic behaviour are perhaps a more direct measure of the failures of vast numbers of young people to become integrated into the social fabric. Yet, according to as conservative a critic as E. D. Hirsch (1987), whose prescription for change is narrow and finite, 'the basic goal of education in a human community is acculturation' (p. xiv).

While the authors of this chapter would not assign blame for social ills to what goes on in schools, they do acknowledge the general expectation that schools should address, if not remedy, those problems. We suggest that all students must first be *engaged* in the act of learning for the healing process, and therefore the learning process, to begin. Many researchers recognize the limited ability of the traditional literary canon to effect such a change. For the canon, according to Michelle Cliff (1988: 59) has served only to bleach the minds of ethnic groups. It institutionalizes and ossifies the world its creators and pre-servers control. Yet literature should be a vehicle whereby students find their place in the world. It is, in a very real sense, 'equipment for living'. Many scholars and practitioners argue for the provision of literary experiences which will enable students to 'make sense of their worlds', individually and collec-tively, and to 'see through the manipulations of all sorts of texts in all sorts of media' (Scholes, 1985: 15–16). It is our belief that adolescent literature can provide this opportunity for all students, especially the disenfranchised. For such students, Merle Hodge's *Crick Crack Monkey* (1981) may be far more appropriate reading than *Jane Eyre* or *Little Women*.

Many voices echo the need for a multicultural perspective in this endeavour. Ong (1982) notes that 'since cultures organize experience and consciousness variously, the study of the literature of another culture opens new vistas both into the exterior world and into the human heart' (p. 3). Others warn of the consequences of not providing relevant literary experiences, noting the pow-erlessness which results from exclusion and the devastating effects on students' sense of self where this occurs (Fetterley, 1978: xiii). A corrective to that consequence is found in works such as Katherine Paterson's *Lyddie* (1991), which chronicles the title character's resilience, faced with adversity.

One reason for the reluctance of some conservatives to embrace the genre is that adolescent literature addresses real issues – coming of age, growing up poor, survival in a hostile world, family strife, discrimination, for example, often from a multicultural perspective. But it is these very qualities which provide young readers with pleasurable reading experiences and create a 'society of readers'. While it encourages personal reading habits, this genre develops in students the confidence, ability and experience required for tackling more mature material (Nugent, 1984: 37). Probst (1987: 27) observes that adolescent literature offers opportunities to 'synthesize knowledge about . . . values, . . . beliefs, . . . relationships with other people and with the world.' Whatever the issue – race relations (Gus Lee, 1991, *China Boy*), prejudice (Uri Orlev, 1991, *The Man from the Other Side*), self-worth (Will Hobbs, 1989, *Bearstone*), coping with disability (Lynn Hall, 1990, *Halsey's Pride*), goals attainment against great odds (Alden Carter, 1989, *Up Country*) – the genre provides rich examples.

The transitional value of this material cannot be overstated, either for skills acquisition or for personal growth. Adolescent novels can bridge the gap for young readers as they learn to experience emotionally and intellectually the material they read. As a stepping stone to more complex material, this genre prevents students' being overwhelmed by vocabulary, syntax, and other substantive demands, according to Nugent (1984). However, Probst (1987) warns against teaching adolescent literature merely as preparation for more difficult canonical works, citing the danger in presuming adolescent novels to be simply rehearsal for 'the real thing', instead of genuine literary experiences *per se* (p. 29). Many titles classified as adolescent literature are, in fact, written for a general audience. Lorene Cary's *Black Ice* (1991), an autobiographical account of growing up gifted and black, is one such. While some critics feel that the study of adolescent literature may postpone students' initiation into the classics, others see the genre as an ideal mode for introducing literary concepts. In addition to providing examples of basic elements, such as plot, characterization and theme, teachers may incorporate study of such complex concepts as critical approaches to literature. Van der Staay (1992) makes a convincing case for applying M. H. Abrams' critical schema to Hinton's *The Outsiders* (1967), for example.

While skill development, including the acquisition of formal conventions for apprehending elements of style and meaning, is essential for developing life-long reading habits, it is in the realm of personal growth that adolescent literature makes its strongest contribution to students' development. The vicarious experience it affords enables students to identify with other peers experiencing problems similar to their own. Many young people may resolve their own dilemmas after examining alternative solutions presented in adolescent literature. David Lisman (1989) observes that 'the serious world that our youths confront cannot be diminished . . . by encouraging them to read . . . works that skirt their own concerns . . . [R]eading works about their own experiences does not . . . [encourage] adolescents to wallow in the slough of . . . adolescence. Rather [it encourages] them to deal with their concerns so *that they can mature.*' (p. 16; the author's italics) In addition to its therapeutic value, the recreational value of such reading is obvious – young people tend to find it interesting. And since adolescent literature is generally more accessible for those in need of skills remediation, it is the ideal vehicle for that purpose. Jan Fisher's poll of young readers (1984) confirms the value of these assertions. Students in this study cited the emotive content, realistic situations, credible style, common problems, and the ability of the material to evoke empathy and insight as reasons for their interest in the genre.

In spite of its utility, many raise objections to classroom use of this body of material, beyond its non-canonical status. In the United States, fundamentalists challenge it for the inclusion of 'violence, cruelty, or sex, particularly . . . deviant sexuality' (Bernstein, 1984: 6) Others attack all books which show youth in conflict with authority, those portraying disrespect for parents, and those which challenge the traditional family structure or question the absolute value of patriotism (Gabler and Gabler, 1982). Some teachers express concerns about novels addressing such issues as 'suicide, mental illness, death, child abuse, or premarital sex', citing the potential harm they could do to impressionable readers (O'Donnell, 1984: 85). It is interesting that Angelotti (1981) finds few texts which are criticized for their writing quality.

So teachers who incorporate adolescent literature are wise to tread carefully, selecting material appropriate for student needs and community standards, and structuring activities which address personal, social and academic goals. But they should not hesitate to capitalize on the genre's merits. Adolescent literature can provide the avenue both for eventual acculturation and for academic success. As Joan Clanchy, Head of North London Collegiate School, acknowledges, 'Enjoyment of books improves reading . . . (*The Independent*, 5/3/93, p. 9). Teachers will succeed to the extent that they can incorporate both knowledge and pleasure into the experience of reading (Herber and Nelson-Herber, in Purves, 1984: 174). To paraphrase Horace, those who blend the useful with the agreeable realize many benefits. Literature which, in Probst's words, 'invites us to participate in the ongoing dialogue of the culture' (p. 27) contributes to students' academic, social and personal growth. Adolescent literature appears especially well suited to inviting that participation.

11 Whose voice is my voice when I write in academe?

SHARON HAMILTON

Calvin is a little boy, about 6 years old, who dwells in Bill Watterson's popular Calvin and Hobbes cartoon strip in North America. As he sorts through the mysteries of his child's world, Calvin talks to his toy tiger, Hobbes, with a cynical sophistication that belies his years. One of those mysteries is the power and use of language. In one recent strip, he says to Hobbes, whom he envisions as a real tiger with both human and animal characteristics:

> 'I like to verb words.'
> 'What?' queries Hobbes.
> 'I take nouns and adjectives and use them as verbs. Remember when "access" was a thing? Now it's something you **do**. It got verbed,' responds Calvin. 'Verbing weirds language.'
> Hobbes, with one of his customarily dry responses, concludes, 'Maybe we can eventually make language a complete impediment to understanding.'

Even if you wince at your recollections of all the nouns that have been 'verbed' in the past decade, you can empathize with Calvin's glee as he discovers he can play with language' to make it do what he wants it to do. In the following strip, Calvin takes his playfulness and control of language even further:

> Sitting at a table, moving pencil across page, he says to Hobbes, 'I used to hate writing assignments, but now I enjoy them. I realized that the purpose of writing is to inflate weak ideas, obscure poor reasoning, and inhibit clarity. With a little practice, writing can be an intimidating and impenetrable fog.' He holds his paper out to Hobbes, 'Want to see my book report?'
> Hobbes reads, 'The Dynamics of Interbeing and Monological Imperatives in *Dick and Jane*: A Study in Psychic Transrelational Gender Modes.'
> Listening to his jargon-laden polysyllabic script, Calvin cheers, 'Academia, here I come!'

Laugh may turn quickly to groan at the thought of how our students often view academic discourse as this stodgy, dense, almost undecipherable prose, and at the traditions of teaching that have formed and perpetuated the rhetorical abuses evident in so much academic writing. Echoing Calvin's discovery and development of control over his voice, particularly in the context of his schooling, this chapter will trace the evolution of my own voice in academia, and will consider how recent pedagogical developments may enhance our students' awareness of and control over the development of their writing voice.

I used to think I was a good writer, though I was never quite certain what good writing entailed. For many years, I thought my writing was considered good because I spelled correctly, used a range of sentence structures, and determinedly incorporated the words from vocabulary lessons into the more extended writing tasks we had. Before I began to write, I planned every main idea, every supporting detail, and the content of every sentence. Schooling acculturated me to the notion, first, that every question asked was answerable, and second, that every answer could be broken down into three major aspects, and each major aspect into three subordinate aspects, with each subordinate aspect supported by the virtually irreproachable evidence of three illustrative details. Confident that even the most limited knowledge of a topic could be organized clearly, coherently and seemingly authoritatively, I dutifully mastered the 'say-what-you're-going-to-say; say-it; say-what-you've-said' formula.

Not until an honours literature class at the University of Winnipeg did I begin to suspect that something might be wrong with my writing, and even that nick in my smugness came in the form of an inverted compliment. Sharing our term papers in preparation for exams, several classmates praised my papers as excellent study aids. They were 'so thorough', 'so organized', 'so easy to follow', *but* – and here the sincere brow of one of my friends furrowed – 'lacking in passion', 'lacking in conviction', lacking in – although we didn't have the language to express it at the time – voice.

Several years later, Harold Rosen, my tutor at the University of London, put it more bluntly. He was responding to the first bit of writing I had produced for my doctoral studies, an assignment that had challenged my learned acceptance of the authority of published experts by requiring me to refute their arguments. With a tired sigh, he growled 'You can get by in the world of academia with this third person objective word-from-God North American dialect if you want to' – he paused to enable me to absorb this assault on my carefully pruned prose – 'but why would you want to? I have no sense of you in here, of you as a reader, of you as a writer, or of you as a teacher. You don't say why you think what you are writing about is important, or why you even took on board the concept to write about in the first place. It's good; it's comprehensive and thorough, even original, and definitely worthy of publication [and it *was* published] but you can do better.'

A few days later, John Dixon, reading the same piece, expressed a related concern. 'Sharon, you let the form do your thinking for you. All of your ideas are subjected to – submissive to – the form. What if you have an idea that just doesn't conform to the tidy organizational structure that controls your writing?'

The resultant 'Aha! Now, finally, I think I understand!' has remained with me and has influenced every aspect of how I write and of how I teach writing. These three comments spaced over several years – no traces of passion, no traces of individuality, no traces of reflective inquiry or genuine conviction, just comprehensive, lucid and rigidly disciplined organization of a rhapsody of ideas, primarily the ideas of other people, of 'authorities' – came together to engender an image that returns whenever I set out to write. That image is a tiny human creature diving into an ocean of ideas, sinking into the flux, struggling to find a path to the surface, treading water for some time while looking all around, then taking firm strokes in a definite direction. The process of that image could be assigned the metaphor 'finding my voice in academe'.

And, in part, that would be correct.

For while I am treading water, I am listening to voices (and if that isn't a mixed – or actually deliberately combined – metaphor, I'm losing my voice as an English teacher). I'm feeling out the various currents of the issue or idea I am exploring; I am considering the dominant voices; the favoured voices; and the silent or silenced voices; and coming to realize the voices furthest from and closest to my own position. That realization becomes the catalyst for striking out in a particular direction, for once I realize which voices are closest to and furthest from my own, I can determine what I will give voice to in my writing. Then I can stroke forcefully in a specific direction, or, to switch to the dominant metaphor, speak with a genuinely authoritative (or genuinely tentative, as the case may be) voice in my own writing.

Therein lies the crux of my 'in part' because the image I described involves choosing one of the many voices with which I speak – the most appropriate one for a particular writing task – rather than the more monolithic challenge of 'finding my own voice' as though I had only one and, somehow, it had gone missing. However, in order to be able to choose among my several voices, I need first to be aware of them as options available to me in my academic writing, and then to be confident that the one I choose will be worth listening to.

So it is with our students.

Almost twenty years ago, James Britton and his research colleagues in the London Schools Council wrote that most of the writing of secondary school children in England was for the teacher-as-examiner. Britton labelled this writing 'dummy runs', since there was no genuine rhetorical context beyond the need to write a paper for a course. Students writing for the teacher-as-examiner were acculturated into a kind of academic discourse that was characteristically agentless ('it can be concluded that . . .' rather than 'I concluded . . .'); allegedly 'projective' ('the facts prove . . .' rather than 'these facts that I selected suggest . . .'); and decidedly voiceless.

Decidedly voiceless? Perhaps not quite. As I write this, I remember a former colleague who taught all of her students to begin every essay with the phrase, 'It is necessary to discuss . . .' In so far as I could recognize her instructional voice in the essays of these students when they entered my classroom the following year, their writing could be said to have voice. But whose voice? Not a thoughtfully chosen academic or personal voice, since they were merely parroting their former teacher's stock phrases and organizational patterns; not her voice, because her own writing was much more original and exciting. And as I sweepingly decry this form-dominated academic discourse as 'voiceless', I must also acknowledge that even writing to form within the most limited constraints reveals to teachers the unique characteristics of each student's voice. We English teachers share the common experience of reading a paper with no name on it and, within a few lines, knowing exactly which of our students has written it. To the extent that any paper 'speaks' in such a way as to reveal its author, it has voice.

All student writing, in that sense, has voice, whether it be a form-dominated, convention-driven academic voice, a voice carefully acquiescent – or consciously resistant – to forms and conventions, or a voice as yet unsteady in forms and conventions, but nevertheless with something significant to say. Student writing is never truly voiceless; it can, however, be without the genuinely authoritative or tentative or playful or reflective voice appropriate to the particular demands of a particular writing task.

We hear our students talking, arguing, cajoling and teasing, inside and outside the classroom, and we know the several voices in their repertoire. How can we help them draw upon these already developed language resources appropriately and effectively in their writing? How can we introduce new elements of discourse to extend these language resources?

The complex relationship between oral and written discourse holds the key; curricular and pedagogical developments may provide the unlocking mechanism. We have all enjoyed the occasional success of asking a student to express orally a thought that he or she has jumbled in writing, and having that student articulate the intended thought clearly and succinctly. At the same time, we know that writing text for unseen, often unknown, readers makes quite different language demands on our students. Enabling our students to develop control in writing over the many voices they already use in their speaking is much more than a matter of primary transcription. It is a matter dependent upon classroom organization, curriculum, assignments and assessment that will both validate and extend their many voices.

Several recent approaches to language teaching have been shown to help students write with increasing competence and confidence. Whole language, collaborative learning, writing across the curriculum, interactive pedagogies, portfolio assessment: all have contributed to reshaping our view of English language classrooms, curricula and textbooks; all have contributed to more equitable sharing of whose voices are heard in the classroom. I have drawn from many of these movements in English language teaching to develop some classroom procedures that, according to my students, enable them to write with a stronger awareness of their own voices:

> At last! I can do it! I can 'hear' myself in this last paper. I can hear myself think, and it's my thinking.
>
> Cindy

> This is the first writing class where I could actually write what was on my mind. Or that I even had something on my mind to write about. Usually I just wrote what I thought the teacher wanted me to write. Now I write what I want to write in relation to audience and purpose.
>
> Danny

> Hey, no shit, man, I can slam dunk it with you like I can in the 'hood. Just kidding. Just trying to check if we really can write with our soul and voice, and not just to fit the teacher's pattern.
>
> Mike

The following procedures represent strategies that my students have pointed out in their journals and course evaluations as being helpful in enabling them to see themselves as writers with something important to say, and with the ability and the voice to say it appropriately and effectively.

1. *Formulating and articulating their own objectives.* Just as we have objectives in mind when we plan a course, our students also have goals for that course, ranging from figuring out how to get through the course with maximum reward for minimum effort, to how to get a date with that pretty redhead or handsome hunk across the aisle, to finding genuine links between what they learn and the lives they lead. Before I introduce my course objectives, I ask my students to write what they hope to achieve in the class. They then form groups to share their goals, and discuss how they might go about achieving them; then, as a class, we talk about them in relation to my goals. Within the first half hour of their first class, their individual voices have begun to make a mark on the organization of the class.

2. *Developing a shared metadiscourse about expectations.* I mentioned earlier that I never fully understood what was meant by 'good writing' in school. My lack of explicit awareness of what constitutes 'good writing' is shared by many of our students. They view the teacher as having the key to all the mysteries, while remaining largely unaware of all the tacit knowledge of language they have acquired through years of reading, writing and speaking. During the first or second class period, I ask each student to list ten features of 'good writing'. I then ask them, in pairs, to negotiate one common list of ten features. Then pairs meet with pairs, once again to negotiate one common list of ten. This continues until the whole class is engaged in one common discussion of features of good writing. The final list forms the shared metadiscourse for the community of writers that the class will become. All of the categories and terms have come from the students, showing them right from the start that their voices are playing a significant curricular role in the class.

3. *Authority and wish lists.*   Early in the term I have my students make two authority lists: a list of things that they do well and a list of their writing strengths; and two wish lists: a list of things they wish to learn more about and a list of aspects of their writing they would like to improve. Because students seldom see themselves as authorities on anything that might be valued within the school culture, they are amazed as their authority lists develop; and, because students seldom envision school as a place where their wishes are seriously considered, they are even more amazed when they are invited to talk about their wish lists in groups to discuss what sorts of writing activities may help them achieve their wishes. Once again their voices are affirmed as significant in their learning.

4. *Valuing each other's voices.*   Paradoxically, though peers influence so much of our students' behaviour, they nevertheless pay more attention to what their teachers say than to what their fellow students say in class discussions. I've seen too many so-called 'class discussions' during which each student comment is solicited by and mediated through the teacher, often repeated by the teacher, and even occasionally rephrased in the teacher's own discourse. It does not take long for students to realize that their way of talking is less valued than their teacher's way. The I-R-E format – (teacher) Initiation → (student) Response → (teacher) Evaluation – is well-documented in classroom-based research, and we all know what happens when everything we say is evaluated. We contribute nothing unless specifically asked, and our voices echo the evaluator's expressed values. A few moves can change that pattern. If a teacher refrains from repeating or rewording what students contribute to the discussion, listens attentively to each student's comments without making evaluative remarks, and then waits for another student to respond instead of jumping right in with his or her own response, students will soon pick up those cues and begin to listen to and respond to each other during class discussions.

5. *Collaborative learning.*   More than any other single pedagogical development in the past twenty-five years, collaborative learning has validated students' voices in the social construction of knowledge within the classroom. Collaborative learning has been shown to break down barriers of race, gender and age as it challenges students to engage more actively and constructively with the concepts of their subject areas. Key elements to establishing collaborative learning environments include enabling students to develop a repertoire of ways to contribute to and benefit from collaborative groups, as well as helping them to develop a system to monitor their contributions and benefits. Voice builds on voice as students talk about their ideas, work to find solutions to problems, negotiate differences of opinion, and discover that each can contribute to and learn from the ideas of their peers.

6. *Formulating writing assignments.*   No greater opportunity exists to nurture – or to squelch – the development of voice in student writing than in the formulation of writing assignments. Every time I read a batch of papers, each of which captures my interest and elicits enthusiastic response, I celebrate the

joy of having hit the mark with my writing assignment; each time I plough laboriously through a batch of dull, disengaged prose, I deplore the realization that I am suffering my own ineptitude in formulating a meaningful writing assignment. The closer a student comes to a real world rhetorical context – something written for someone other than the teacher, for a purpose important to, and preferably chosen by, the student, in a genre and voice appropriate to that purpose, and then *the paper is actually used for that purpose* – the more exciting, engaged, and powerful the writing is, and the more enjoyable it is for me to read.

7. *Negotiating assessment.*   When students view assessment as a one-way street from teacher to student, they know that their voices have been silenced in a significant arena of their writing, and even of their schooling. When students participate in the assessment process, especially in formative kinds of assessment, their voices can contribute significantly to their own learning. I have found letters of transmittal and response particularly helpful for involving students in formative assessment of their writing. Whenever students hand in a 'final' version of their paper, they accompany it with a letter of transmittal. In this letter they tell me whatever they consider salient about the process of composing the paper, the areas they feel good about, areas they feel uncomfortable with, anything different or unusual that they attempted, and particular features of their writing that they particularly want me to respond to or comment on as I read their papers. The process of writing these letters in itself heightens students' awareness of their own strengths and weaknesses, and reveals to me immediately the level and focus of their concerns, thereby aiding us both. After students read my responses to their papers, they write me their reactions to my response, letting me know what they agree and disagree with, what I might have left out that they particularly wanted to know, what they don't understand and need direct help with, or anything else that they consider pertinent. These letters enable my students to add their voices to my reading of and responses to their writing.

8. *Portfolio assessment.*   Portfolio assessment is one of the most promising recent developments in assessment, especially in relation to students' developing their range and control over voice in writing. In the short term, when portfolios represent the work of several months or a school year, students and teachers both have an opportunity to examine the range of writing done, the variety of rhetorical contexts, and the voices that speak within them. When students select the pieces to include, decide upon their arrangement within the portfolio and write a letter of transmittal guiding readers through it, they find themselves drawn to certain kinds of their writing over others. In discovering relationships among rhetorical context, voice, and writing preferences, especially if they work together in collaborative groups to discern and discuss these relationships, students significantly broaden their understanding of their own and of each other's voices in writing. In the long term, when portfolios represent work done over a period of several years, students have an unparalleled

opportunity to trace the development of their dominant voice, the birth of new voices, and the path of maturation away from earlier voices.

9. *Assessing the assessors.* Although most of what I have written above has evolved from a combination of classroom experience, professional reading, collegial conversations, and conferences, the adjustments and refinements that have occurred in my classroom have been largely motivated by my students. Every course every semester is evaluated by every student. Not only do students acutely home in on weaknesses or inconsistencies, they often make excellent suggestions for modifications. When I point out to students particular features of the course requirements or course procedures that were inspired or suggested by former students, I am implicitly telling them that they have a significant voice in shaping their learning environment.

What all of the above procedures and strategies add up to is the assertion that expecting students to develop an authentic and confident voice in their writing compels us to provide opportunities for them to use their voices throughout the entire infrastructure of their learning environment. We too often suppose that students will somehow develop an 'authentic voice' through excellent writing instruction, while not supporting this development with opportunities for their authentic voices to shape the design of their educational context. When writing is used primarily to demonstrate to a teacher-as-examiner what students already know, the expectation for voice in that writing is a knowledgeable, authoritative voice presenting facts and supporting evidence in an allegedly objective manner. When writing is used to discover what we may know, or to make sense of experiences, facts, and opinions or to tease out an idea, to reflect, to wander the paths of linguistic dalliance, to learn more about who we are and what we believe, we correspondingly develop appropriate voices to accommodate these diverse demands on our language resources.

In raising the question, 'Whose voice is my voice when I write in academe?' I am not intentionally creating a tautology. I am intending that the phrase 'in academe' be sufficiently indeterminate to suggest the physical space of an educational institution; the conceptual space of intellectual inquiry; the semiotic space of a kind of academic dialect or discourse. When our students write 'in academe' they simultaneously confront the challenge of negotiating meaning in all three spaces. The easiest path to follow is the one set by their teacher's voice and language values. Their voice in academe then becomes a junior echo of the teacher's, an echo that has reverberated from generation to generation throughout the history of schooling. Current understanding of thought, language, and voice, coupled with growing acknowledgement and appreciation of linguistic and cultural diversity, opens many alternate routes to negotiate the physical, intellectual and linguistic spaces of academia. Working together, students and teachers can employ their voices collectively and individually, consensually and personally, harmoniously and discordantly as they struggle to construct and articulate meaning in their day-by-day study of the academic universe.

12 English in its place

BEVERLEY BRYAN

English as cultural transmission

Franz Fanon (1968) in his examination of the psychological damage of colonialism points to language as a key instrument in the process by which the individual can become dominated by another culture:

> To speak means to be in a position to use a certain syntax, to grasp the morphology of this or that language but it means above all to assume a culture, to support the weight of a civilisation.
>
> (p. 13)

With such a statement Fanon makes the function of language as cultural transmission paramount and absolute. Predictably, native speakers of English see English teaching generally in this vein, as deeply ideological and inextricably bound to the culture and values of English society. This perspective informs Cameron and Bourne's (1989) critique of the Kingman Report (1988) which they see as reinforcing a perception of English as the prized possession of a great nation. Such a definition of the English curriculum is also obliquely acknowledged by Brian Griffiths (*The Sunday Times*, 17/1/93) in 'matters such as literacy and heritage'. These are the expected concerns of those whose primary language is English, who work in a first language environment of English as a Native Language (ENL) and who would seek, first and foremost, to define the concerns and preoccupations of an English curriculum.

Teachers with a similar language background have taken these same preoccupations abroad, to the experience of English as a Second Language and Foreign Language (ESL and EFL), and have been similarly uneasy about the ideas teachers carry to, and the students take from, their language classrooms. Rogers (1990) makes a wide-ranging attack on the ideological implications of English teaching abroad. Apart from challenging the efficacy of English as the route to upward mobility in the Third World, he questions the notion of the importance of English universally as an international language, arguing that only a very small number of people need to use it for communication purposes.

He is particularly concerned about its automatic linkages with science, technology, development and progress. In going on to quote Freire, he equates the teaching of English with education itself and points to its dominant integrative tendency which constrains 'the practice of freedom'.

What Cameron and Bourne, and Rogers portray is an English teaching that is fundamentally compromised in its delivery to both first and second language learners: a language which, because of its ideological import, inevitably contaminates its learners. From their analysis, no country can have a national policy to promote the English language and retain a vibrant culture untainted by the beliefs and orthodoxies which govern English society.

This is the position which is to be examined here. It should be stated that it is a position refuted (in the same volume as Rogers) by Alptekin and Alptekin, who give a general review of countries such as Japan, China and Kuwait where attempts are being made to divest English teaching of those alien features which make the language unacceptable, by defining 'the possibility of becoming bilingual without becoming bicultural' (p. 23). Such a stance is, of course, feasible if English and the other language are seen unquestionably as separate and different, where English can be viewed as a Foreign Language, and where primary language acquisition, as the first channel of cultural transmission, may counter later negative influences. Such a stance is also possible where the two societies can attempt to interact without a sociocultural history of domination and oppression. This is not the case with the Caribbean, with its complex and stormy relationship with English history and the English language. In this specific context the question of how an ex-colony continues to use English as its official language and still maintains its linguistic integrity will be examined with specific reference to Jamaica.

The case of Jamaica: the language situation

The sociolinguistic situation in Jamaica is informed by its history of slavery and colonialism. The West African slave population of primarily Twi descent (Alleyne, 1989) brought with them a language which, through interaction with the limited English of overseers and those of that class involved in those desperate settings, formed the basis of an evolving new language, Jamaican Creole (JC). The stabilized new language reflected the political dominance of English in that its lexicon was English. It also drew on the West African dominance of Twi-Asante as one of the first major African languages on the island. Some would concede a third factor expounded by Bickerton (1981) and include a universalistic Creole-making trigger.

With such a dynamic and complex history, characterizations of the language situation have employed different explanatory procedures. The classic definition of diglossia (Ferguson, 1972) which purports a common, Low language used by all, with a distinct High variety reserved for prestigious situations, has sometimes been applied (Hudson, 1980). This remains problematic as the diglossic template can be used only in a situation where the two forms of speech are seen as quite closely related and no more than variants of each other. Most importantly, JC speakers operate in conditions where all aspects of the language situation are fluid. Concepts of what constitutes a language are changing even as the concept of diglossia is also developing (Hudson, 1980; Devonish, 1986). Additionally, and most importantly, problems will arise in pin-pointing the situations for using the different varieties as there will be shifts in the social patterns themselves, which dictate language use.

An alternative model to characterize the language situation in Jamaica is that of the continuum. Exclusive Creole, the basilect, uninfluenced by schooling or society and associated with the deep, rural areas, would be at one end of the continuum, with the standard Jamaican English (SJE) of the urban middle class at the other. In between those idealized extremes would be all the mesolectal varieties actually used, with speakers moving along the continuum, according to situation or class. There would be very few cases where the speaker could produce only one variety and thus DeCamp's (1971a) explanation still has validity in indicating that the wider the social network of contacts, the greater the need for flexibility and movement along the continuum. The politician who wishes to remain successful has to shift endlessly from one band of speech to another.

Language education in Jamaica

In spite of this flexibility and fluidity in speech, it cannot be denied that schools are expected to produce undisputed Standard English in writing: there is no Jamaican Standard when it comes to examinations. The lively debates which have continued in the press about the benefits of Creole become acrimonious when discussion turns to the number of examination passes in English obtained by Jamaican schoolchildren and the standard of English of entrants to the university. The clear indication is that the main sphere of concern is with English as the language of business, academic life and international discourse. With such support for English it might be said that society has taken on the 'weight of a civilization' as propounded by Fanon, and that in an attempt to promote English, the other language has been ignored. This, however, is not the case in Jamaica. In order to see how its society has managed to keep English in its place, it is necessary to examine the concept of English as an international language from a Caribbean perspective.

English as an international language

The re-statement comes from Carrington (1988a) who, as a language educator in the Caribbean, attempts to wrench English from a geographical location and establish it firmly as an international language which has to function independently of the society from which it came:

An international language is not the possession of a specific group. It is public property. It is not the vehicle of a single culture. It becomes the vehicle of any culture to which a user applies it.

Carrington makes the case for all those in a Caribbean setting who might want to learn a language categorized as international, without necessarily seeking membership of the society from which it came, or ownership of the manners and mores associated with it. He credits these learners with some volition and sees that they would wish to use that language for their own varied purposes. This perspective would have implications for language teaching, with a re-orientation away from an unexamined cultural imposition of ideas conveyed in such items as the use of metaphor and choice of literature, and towards a closer scrutiny of what constitutes peripheral knowledge to the teaching of English and what has to be maintained as the essential core.

In making this case, Carrington is taking an unashamedly instrumentalist position, asserting the possibility for societies to learn an a-cultural English for their own purposes, be they academic, financial or otherwise, and still to maintain their own separate culture. As indicated earlier, Alptekin and Alptekin described such a stance as possible for those countries having distinct and unambiguous independence from the source of English. Carrington is making the case for that same kind of relationship in the Caribbean context also, where there are long linguistic and cultural linkages.

The proposition of bilingualism without the concomitant effect of unbal-anced biculturalism is not, however, just based on a simple assertion of English as an international language. There are, in Jamaica, a number of major social and cultural indications of an emergent self-confidence and growth, which can be discussed here. One such indicative factor is the changing attitude towards the vernacular language.

Changing attitudes: changing patterns

During the first Creole Conference, DeCamp (1971b) could record the nega-tive attitudes of the general population towards the vernacular language. It was seen as 'inseparably associated with poverty, ignorance and lack of moral character' (p. 26). This can be linked with the political environment, where subject peoples with little sense of their own culture take on the values and ideas of the dominant culture. Some of these views still prevail among pro-fessional letter writers to the editor, who might describe Creole as 'inadequate (for thought) despite all claims to its expressiveness' (*The Daily Gleaner*, 31/12/90). Nevertheless, attitudes towards the language have shifted perceptibly in many spheres. It is now seen as a serious object of study and an important part of the cultural repertoire of the people, rather than a Low variety of English. In the academic field, new areas have been mapped out which have succeeded in bringing research into the popular public domain. Research into the African substrate influences (e.g. Alleyne, 1980) has established a lineage previously obscured by the lexical relationship of the Creole to English. Descriptions of new formulations coming out of indigenous cultural formations such as the Rastafari movement (Pollard, 1983a) have confirmed the possibilities of the language to re-make itself. Arguments for extending the official uses of Creole in public life (Devonish, 1986) have stimulated the debate beyond notions of mere adequacy and expressiveness.

Perhaps the most decisive and expanded use of the Creole voice has been that examined by Shields (1989, 1992), who has been investigating Creole use in the media. Radio, rather than newspapers, is the source of information and political discussion. The talk show, which has taken on a global prominence, typically figures as an opportunity for the free expression of Jamaican Creole (JC). Shields records that news broadcasts have shifted from their tendency to summarize and paraphrase the ideas of ordinary people which would have, at one time, been dismissed as incoherent, to allowing those involved in the stories to speak for themselves. In these reports, citizens have complained about their local conditions and commented on international events, operating in a linguistic milieu usually reserved for speakers of Standard Jamaican English (SJE).

This situation shows that, despite the long history of domination of psychological inferiority, the movement towards recognition has surely and optimistically begun. The emerging self-confidence is not only that of the original speakers of Creole but also of the opinion-makers in society who are beginning to accept the notion of the continuum. It is really a self-assurance, a nascent awareness of what might be the wider linguistic choices and resources available to people.

The Standard reassessed

Mirroring the changing attitudes and practices at the basilectal end of the continuum, Shields (1989) highlights a development in the representation at the acrolectal end. She unpicks the model of idealized Standard Jamaican English to revise it, in line with what is actually being used, demonstrating that a new standard is emerging, in consistent use by those with post-secondary education. It is a form of language that could be described as adoptive rather than native, a Standard learnt passively in written form rather than through active use. It is, consequently, unable to shift from formal to informal styles, producing a one-dimensional register. The suggestion is of a kind of local English, competing with the traditional Standard. Pollard (1992) adds a new dimension to this emerging standard, by directing us towards the continuing infiltration of Dread Talk (DT) and its transforming effect on accepted forms. She documents the ongoing process by which the language of the Rastafari leavens the lexicon of the educated minority. She shows that, unconsciously, a number of words are being used which, although superficially English, have taken on new meanings from DT (e.g. *trod* and *penetrate*).

We know how long he has been *trodding* here in Jamaica. (Female director of government agency at book launch.)

I was late because I wasn't *penetrating* the time. (Messenger to lecturer in an otherwise English conversation.)

The purest form of Standard English is being replaced by something that cannot be so precisely described in terms of phonology and morphology and also in terms of syntax. As is happening in many parts of the world (cf. Omodiaogbe, 1992 on Nigeria), the use of Standard English is undergoing structural change, and is becoming nativized. In Jamaica, all these factors question the uni-directionality of decreolization as propounded by such as DeCamp and attest to profound changes in the attitude towards English.

Changing attitudes to English

The change in attitude to what was the dominant language is another factor in our discussion of the national language policy. As early as the poetry of Louise Bennett (1966), there was some subversive undermining of the role of English. In 'Poor Gum' she decries the 'gum mal-treatment' she witnessed, in the assault on the English language, at a 1940s Fabian Society conference in England. In 'Dry Foot Bwoy' the focus is on the returning migrant who has too quickly adopted English pronunciation, to much derision in his home district. These are the early indications that the English language is seen as something alien to the lives of the people, affected with the mark of otherness, which, as in Nigeria, is sometimes characterized as the language of the 'been to', the returnee from foreign parts. A locally produced Jamaican soap opera 'Lime Tree Lane', has, as its most popular character a snobbish lady named Mrs Upton/Uptown who is prone to torturing the English language in a bid to master its syntax. She is unquestionably a figure of fun. What is being suggested here is that language, continuing on an evolutionary path in a country such as Jamaica, is much more fluid than in many other countries. So, although it remains primarily an English as a Second *Dialect* environment, with a certain insistence on Standard English for writing, there is a tendency towards functioning with more duality, as if in an English as a Second *Language* environment. This has tremendous ramifications for further raising the status of Creole.

Privileging the voice

Right along the creative spectrum of the performing arts, JC functions as the natural language, expressing the national aspirations of the people. One such example of this self-confident development is in the area of poetry. Early Creole poetry was acceptable in a humorous vein because it was seen that only certain kinds of issues and topics could be dealt with in the language of the people (Craig, 1976). Louise Bennett took one small step to change this but, as Rohlehr (1989) indicates, the debate about the potential of Creole languages to sustain the crafted words and philosophical ideas of poetry has now been resolved. He acknowledges the value of the concept of the continuum and links it with the aesthetic spectrum of the oral tradition which includes 'a virtually limitless range of prosodic, rhetorical, and musical shapes' (p. 2). In the collection *Voiceprint*, Brown *et al.* include legends, laments, sermons, calypsos, tracings, praisesongs and all manner of voice compositions. The language continuum parallels the oral tradition and allows us to examine the work of a range of poets, from Claude Mackay to Michael Smith, who privilege the voice.

Michael Smith was one of the best exponents of that type of poetry spoken to music known as dub poetry. With its roots in the speech and music of ghetto experience, it has been the site of the most protracted struggle for recognition, primarily because of the politics of its content and its heavy reliance on music to structure its form and on performance to convey its import. This poetry, while not denying the humorous, covers all nuances of feelings and ideas. Consider Mutabaruka's 'Butta Pan' or Michael Smith's 'Mi Cyaan Believe It' or Jean 'Binta' Breeze's 'Riddym Ravings', which are all included in *Voiceprint*. These examples show a strong affirmation of a distinctive and un-English national voice.

Alternative voices

For some it might seem that acceptance of this poetry is part of the co-option of the voice, corralled for prescribed circumstances. This is hardly the case in music, still one of the most vibrant expressions of the language. It is certainly not the case with Dancehall, a fusion of words and music which bears some relationship to dub poetry but which has been stigmatized because of the content of its 'lyrics' and the context of its performance. Like dub poetry, dancehall music was spawned by the DJs, who put their own improvised words to early reggae music at dances which were the most popular form of entertainment in poor urban and rural communities. Dancehall music is significant first because it confirms the efficacy of the two continua, operating at the basilectal end of the language continuum and also at the furthest extreme of the literary oral tradition. Second, it indicates the extent to which a self-confident Jamaica can be said to have moved from English-inclined sensibilities in terms of culture. Third, it illustrates Carrington's (1988b) point about the social dynamics of independence, where the erosion of the old elite base has led to new routes to social acceptability, where DJs can be viewed as role models in the communities from which they came.

Dancehall music has not, however, been accepted so readily outside these communities. This mix of ghetto lifestyle, Creole language and reggae music has routinely been denounced as 'slackness' because of its coarse, sexist and homophobic lyrics. Cooper (1989) makes the case for this expression of the culture:

> it can be seen to represent in part a radical, underground confrontation with the pious morality and conservative gender ideology of fundamentalist Jamaican society . . . Slackness is not mere sexual looseness – though it certainly is that. Slackness is a metaphorical revolt against law and order.
>
> (p. 14)

Irrespective of the criticism directed towards it, dancehall music seems to be able to defend itself on its own confident terms. Lovindeer, a popular DJ in the dancehall style and sometime performer for the Jamaica Information Service (JIS) in its community education metrication drive, put the matter firmly in context:

> In the confines of the dancehall, where anything goes, and for the people who go and want to hear this kind of thing, there's nothing wrong with it. The slacker the lyrics you come up with, the more gun salute and pram-pram you get.
>
> (*Jamaica Journal*, 23: 1)

The message is clear: this music does not need the benediction of the establishment; it has its own mode of delivery to its devotees. Traditional class structures are eroded, allowing alternative models for mobility to thrive: alternative lifestyles and aspirations appear as seductive.

Changing perspectives in education

What has been the impact of this changing sociolinguistic situation on classroom practice? Traditionally, language education in Jamaica has promoted English, by the severest correction, as the only source of learning: the ideological import in the classroom has been strong. However, the changing use and meaning of English have allowed a greater degree of discussion about what should be the most appropriate teaching methods in a society where the possibilities for English have been those of Native Language, Second Dialect or Second Language. Craig (1976), drawing also on the notion of the continuum to examine and explain some of the problems Jamaican children might have in the education system, as it was then constructed, accepted the notion of bidialectalism because of the clear dysjuncture between the school as the predominantly English-speaking environment, and the home and playground where the language in use was JC. One of his greatest concerns was to examine attitudes to the common language and its effect on the educational policies of the country. He recognized, however, that in the bidialectal situation which he described, the changing set of sociolinguistic variables required a new and flexible perspective on language learning. He acknowledged the possibility of a Creole-speaking society achieving total cognitive and aesthetic development through its indigenous language. But because the demand for English was strong, teaching methods had to take this reality into account. Craig (1967) had suggested a kind of audio-lingualism but this was later married to a more communicative approach (1976). Use of such notions as 'free talk' and 'controlled talk' (Craig, 1980) suggests an attempt to validate the home language and bring its fluency into the classroom, thus providing students with greater opportunities to use Creole for oral communication. Craig modified Fishman and Lovas to present a number of different models for language education policies relevant to Jamaica. They were:

1. *Monolingualism in school in the dominant language*: denying the home language.
2. *Transitional bilingualism*: using the home language in an initial period to secure entry to school.
3. *Monoliterate bilingualism*: both languages are developed for oral-aural skills but SE for literacy in school language.
4. *Partial bilingualism*: developing fluency and literacy in certain subjects with the home language, while providing unlimited encouragement for school language.
5. *Full bilingualism*: equal treatment for both languages.
6. *Monolingualism in home language*: the home language as the medium of instruction.

The models represented, with one exception, recommend the inclusion of some Creole in the language education programme. This indicates something of the importance being given to Creole in the education process, whether in oral expression or in creative writing.

What has happened to Craig's models is that different aspects of them have been taken on in the Jamaican schools programme because of the collaborative arrangements that have, at times, been in place between the University of the West Indies and the Ministry of Education. Certainly the exclusive English monolingualism of earlier years no longer obtains. There is a recognition that the different language structures in use and the shifting patterns require different approaches. Pollard (1983b), also recognizing the duality of the language experience, draws on Widdowson addressing an ESL audience and Barnes from a ENL perspective, to emphasize language related to content and the concurrent concern of language across the curriculum.

Both Pollard and Craig would draw on the armoury of EFL/ESL practice to meet the needs of English in the Second Dialect/Language environment. The new proposals coming from the Jamaican Ministry of Education (quoted in the *Journal of English Teachers*, 1992) also acknowledge the complexity of the language situation. They recognize that students will receive few opportunities outside the school to practise the English required inside and so they opt for a communicative approach but include grammar objectives such as 'To know the basic differences between the forms of Creole and Standard English'. Simple as this objective seems, it is a major change in the perception of Creole and the handling of the vernacular language, which consequently changes the treatment of English in the classroom.

In pinpointing this objective, I return obliquely to the initial comments of this chapter. There, English was seen as undifferentiated arbiter of culture. It is true that language is cultural transmission but this can only remain uncontested in cases where the school and home languages coalesce. This is not the case with Jamaica. Certainly, knowledge and use of English continue to be important and, as the medium of instruction, its sphere of influence is fixed for the time being. We can, however, note and perhaps celebrate the cultural changes impacting on the richness and variety of its use, as users seek to uncouple the language from its colonial past. One such example of the divestment of that baggage is the unselfconscious inclusion of Caribbean literature as the bulk of Jamaican English examination syllabuses, responding to what Rohlehr calls 'indigenous sensibilities'. This is only possible in a society which sees its users cherishing its history and culture. It will happen; it does not have to be done for them; they need to be allowed to do it for themselves.

13 Which English – or English *Which?*

DAVID CRYSTAL

'Choice' is one of the buzz-words of the 1990s. We find it frequently mentioned in the publicity statements and charters whereby institutions define their policies to the public. In 1993, for example, the BBC issued a document entitled 'Extending Choice', and introduced a policy of 'Producer Choice'. Shops continue to proclaim the benefits of 'customer choice', and consumer organizations examine the realities beneath these claims. In educational contexts, the notion appears as part of the discussion of curriculum options and in the selection of literary texts.

Choice is also a familiar notion in linguistics, long being part of the analysis of the contrasts presented by a language – for example, the 'choice' between singular and plural, voiced and voiceless, synchronic and diachronic, or syntagmatic and paradigmatic. It is inherent in stylistics, where the language is seen as making available to authors a range of 'choices' (in vocabulary, word order, rhyme, etc.) and it is therefore not surprising to find it looming large in the context of the language curriculum, where there has been a great deal of discussion of the kind of varieties that children should be expected to deal with, and of the range of linguistic features which should be prescribed or proscribed. Indeed, the whole prescriptive/descriptive debate in language teaching could be reformulated as a question of choice: Who decides what language we shall speak or write in our society?

What role should the linguist play, in the educational debate? Responsible choice presupposes an informed awareness of the range from which to choose. The consumer magazine *Which?* describes itself as 'the most comprehensive source of independent, unbiased information about goods and services on offer to consumers in the UK'. This is a satisfactory perspective for linguists also. Which linguistic goods and services are on offer to the English-using child? Linguists can provide both synchronic and diachronic answers to this question. The synchronic issue is one of selection: which varieties and features shall we introduce? The diachronic issue is one of sequence: in which chronological order shall we present these matters to children? This chapter looks only at the synchronic issue, and in particular at the question of Standard English – which, if anything, is what most people want children ultimately to be able to 'own'.

The discussion of the notion of 'standard' varies, depending on whether we are dealing with it at a national or international level. At a national level, in several countries (but especially in the United Kingdom), the concern has focused on its place as part of an acceptable national curriculum for English in primary and secondary education. At international level, the focus has been on the question of which national standards should be used in teaching English as a foreign language. In both contexts, however, before sensible decisions can be made about how to introduce standard English or teach it, there is a need for clear understanding about what it actually is. The cautious opening of the entry on Standard English (SE) in *The Oxford Companion to the English Language* (1992), written by the editor, Tom McArthur, suggests that we may be entering a minefield: 'a widely used term that resists easy definition but is used as if most educated people nonetheless know precisely what it refers to . . .' Disentangling the issues is best done first at national level, where the issues have been around a long time, and are reasonably well understood.

What is Standard English?

From the dozens of definitions available in the literature on English, we may extract five essential characteristics:

- Standard English (SE) is a *variety* of English – a distinctive combination of linguistic features with a particular role to play. Some people call it a 'dialect' of English – and so it is, but of a rather special kind, for it has no local base. There is nothing in the grammar and vocabulary of a piece of SE to tell us which part of a country it comes from.
- The linguistic features of SE are chiefly matters of grammar, vocabulary, and orthography (spelling and punctuation). It is important to note that SE is not a matter of pronunciation: SE is spoken in a wide variety of accents (including, of course, any prestige accent a country may have, such as Received Pronunciation).
- SE is the variety of English which carries most prestige within a country. 'Prestige' is a social concept, whereby some people have high standing in the eyes of others, whether this derives from social class, material success, political strength, popular acclaim, or educational background. The English that these people choose to use will, by this very fact, become the standard within their community. In the words of one US linguist, James Sledd, SE is 'the English used by the powerful'.
- The prestige attached to SE is recognized by adult members of the community, and this motivates them to recommend SE as a desirable educational target. It is the variety which is used as the norm of communication by the

community's leading institutions, such as its government, law courts, and media. It is therefore the variety which is likely to be the most widely disseminated among the public. It will, accordingly, be widely understood – though not by everyone, and with varying comprehension of some of its features (thus motivating the demands of the 'plain English' campaigns). It may or may not be liked.

- Although SE is widely understood, it is not widely produced. Only a minority of people within a country (e.g. radio newscasters) actually use it when they talk. Most people speak a variety of regional English, or an admixture of standard and regional Englishes, and reserve such labels as 'BBC English' or 'the Queen's English' for what they perceive to be a 'pure' SE. Similarly, when they write – itself a minority activity – the consistent use of SE is required only in certain tasks (such as a letter to a newspaper, but not necessarily to an old friend). More than anywhere else, SE is to be found in print.

On this basis, we may define the Standard English of an English-speaking country as a minority variety (identified chiefly by its vocabulary, grammar, and orthography) which carries most prestige and is most widely understood.

The origins of Standard English

This variety is the result of a combination of influences, the most important of which do not emerge until the Middle English period. There is no direct connection between West Saxon, the prestige dialect of Old English and the modern standard. The political heart of the country moved from Winchester to London after the Conquest, and the major linguistic trends during Middle English increasingly relate to the development of the capital as a social, political, and commercial centre. A written Standard English began to emerge during the fifteenth century and, following the detailed study of the dialect characteristics of the period, it is now possible to isolate key factors which contributed to its identity:

- A regionally standardized literary language appeared in the last part of the fourteenth century, based on the dialects of the Central Midland counties, especially Northamptonshire, Huntingdonshire and Bedfordshire. This is chiefly found in the large number of Wycliffite manuscripts which have survived, including sermons, tracts, prayers, poems, and the different versions of the Wycliffe Bible, as well as several secular works. The Lollards spread this variety widely, even into south-west England, thus increasing its status as a standard. In the long term, it was unable to compete with the quantity of material emanating from the capital, but its Central Midland origins are nevertheless noteworthy.
- The growth of a standard from the London area can be seen by the mid-fourteenth century. Although London was very much a dialectal hybrid

(with the City influenced by the Essex dialect, and Westminster, some distance further west, showing the influence of Middlesex), patterns of standardization gradually appear. There is a small group of manuscripts, written prior to 1370, which are noted for their uniformity of spelling. A later and much larger group of diverse manuscripts includes the work of Chaucer and Gower. These texts in their different ways represent London English of around 1400, but the amount of variation they display suggests that they cannot be called a standard, in any strict sense. Not even Chaucer's writing, traditionally thought to be a precursor of modern Standard English, exercised a specific influence on the form this standard took – nor is it likely that poetic usage would ever influence general usage in any real way. It can hardly be doubted, though, that Chaucer's literary standing would have greatly added to the prestige associated with written language in the London dialect.

- The most significant factor must have been the emergence of London as the political and commercial centre of the country. In particular the influence of the administrative offices of the London Chancery is now thought to have been critical, especially after c.1430. Vast amounts of manuscript copying took place within the Westminster area, and standards of practice emerged among the Chancery scribes. These practices then influenced the many individual scribes who worked privately, and eventually all kinds of material, including literary texts, were affected. It would not have taken long for a widespread standardization to be current. When Caxton set up his press, also in Westminster, and chose local London speech as his norm, the lasting influence of his Chancery neighbours was assured.

These observations add up to the claim that the main influence on the standard language was the Central Midlands area, several of whose linguistic features eventually influenced the shape of Chancery Standard. That the central area could exercise such influence is suggested by a number of contemporary comments, as well as by deductions based on social history. John of Trevisa, translating Higden's *Polychronicon* in c.1387, identifies its function as a communication 'bridge' between north and south (*th* here replaces his use of the Old English letter 'thorn'):

> for men of the est with men of the west, as it were vndir the same partie of heuene, acordeth more in sownynge of speche [pronunciation] than men of the north with men of the south; therfore it is that Mercii [Mercians], that beeth men of myddel Engelond, as it were parteners of the endes, vnderstondeth bettre the side langages, northerne and southerne, than northerne and southerne vnderstondeth either other.

By way of social considerations, we have evidence of a marked population shift in the fourteenth century. In the earlier part of that century, immigration to the London area was highest from the East Midlands counties of Norfolk, Essex and Hertfordshire, but it later increased dramatically from such Central

Midlands counties as Leicestershire, Northamptonshire and Bedfordshire. As a result, the London dialect came to display many of the linguistic features of Midland writing.

These observations bring a fresh perspective to the traditional map of Middle English dialects, where no recognition is given to a Central Midlands area, and where special attention is paid to an East Midlands 'triangle' bounded by London, Cambridge, and (on the borders with Southern) Oxford – an area of high population, containing the main social and political centre, and the main seats of learning. This was a wealthy agricultural region, and the centre of the growing wool trade. Its role in promoting the importance of the south-east in the Middle Ages is clear. However, the findings of present-day historical dialectology suggest that its linguistic influence was far less important than that of the area further west.

The final factor in the development of a southern literary standard was the development of printing. This resulted in the spread of a single norm over most of the country, so much so that during the fifteenth century it becomes increasingly difficult to determine on internal linguistic grounds the dialect in which a literary work is written – apart from the northern dialects, such as Scots, which retained their written identity longer. People now begin to make value judgements about other dialects. In the Towneley Plays, Mak the sheep-stealer masquerades as a person of importance, and adopts a southern accent. John of Trevisa comments that northern speech is 'scharp, slitting, and frotynge and vnschape' ('shrill, cutting, and grating and ill-formed'), giving as one of the reasons that northerners live far away from the court. And in *The Arte of English Poesie*, attributed to George Puttenham (c.1520–90), the aspiring poet is advised to use 'the usuall speach of the Court, and that of London and the shires lying about London within lx. myles, and not much above'. There was never to be total uniformity, but the forerunner of Standard English undoubtedly existed by the end of the fifteenth century.

World Standard English?

The history of Standard English in Britain is now fairly well understood. What is difficult is to know what to expect when a language develops a worldwide presence to the extent that English has. There are no precedents for such a geographical spread or for so many speakers. Moreover, the speed at which it has all happened is unprecedented: although the history of world English can be traced back 400 years, the current growth spurt in the language has a history of less than 40 years. There has never been such an increase in independent states (United Nations membership has more than doubled since 1960) nor such a growth in world population (from 2.5 thousand million in 1950 to 5.4 thousand million in 1992). How will English fare (how would *any* language fare?), faced with such responsibilities and having to respond to such pressures?

The two chief issues – internationalism and identity – raise an immediate problem, because they conflict. In the former case, a nation looks out from itself at the world as a whole, and tries to define its needs in relation to that world. In the latter case, a nation looks within itself at the structure of its society and the psychology of its people, and tries to define its needs in relation to its sense of national identity. Corresponding linguistic issues automatically arise:

- *Internationalism implies intelligibility.* If the reason for any nation wishing to promote English is to give it access to what the broader English-speaking world has to offer, then it is crucial for its people to be able to understand the English of that world, and to be understood in their turn. In short, internationalism demands an agreed standard – in grammar, vocabulary, spelling, pronunciation and conventions of use.
- *Identity implies individuality.* If a nation wishes to preserve its uniqueness or to establish its presence, and to avoid being an anonymous ingredient in a cultural melting-pot, then it must search for ways of expressing its difference from the rest of the world. Flags, uniforms and other such symbols will have their place, but nothing will be so naturally and universally present as a national language – or, if there is none, a national variety of an international language. In short, in the context of English, identity demands linguistic distinctiveness – in grammar, vocabulary, spelling, pronunciation, or conventions of language use.

How the English language will develop depends on how the tension between these two principles will be resolved. Currently, the notion of 'standard' cannot be generalized to a world context in a straightforward way. If we read the newspapers or listen to the newscasters around the English-speaking world, we will quickly develop the impression that there is a World Standard English (WSE), acting as a strongly unifying force among the vast range of variation which exists. However, a totally uniform, regionally neutral, and unarguably prestigious variety does not yet exist worldwide.

- Each country where English is a first language is aware of its linguistic identity and is anxious to preserve it from the influence of others. New Zealanders do not want to be Australians; Canadians do not want to be Americans; and 'Americanism' is perceived as a danger signal by usage guardians everywhere (except in America).
- All other countries can be grouped into those which follow American English, those which follow British English, and those (e.g. Canada) where there is a mixture of influences. One of the most noticeable features of this divided usage is spelling. In certain domains, such as computing and medicine, US spellings are becoming increasingly widespread (*program*, *disk*, *pediatrics*), but we are a long way from uniformity.
- A great deal of lexical distinctiveness can be observed in the specialized

terms of local politics, business, culture and natural history, and in the 'domestic' columns of national newspapers (such as 'Want Ads'). There is also a certain amount of grammatical distinctiveness, especially between US and UK English.

- The notion of a 'standard pronunciation' is useful in the international setting of English as a second or foreign language, but here too there is more than one teaching model – chiefly, British Received Pronunciation and US General American.
- The question of prestige is not easy to determine, at an international level, because of the different national histories which co-exist. Would it be more prestigious for a report from an international body to appear in British or American spelling? Should it refer to *cars* or *automobiles*? What image do its authors wish to convey? Decisions about such matters are made in innumerable contexts every day. It will take time before the world sees a consensus, and only time will tell whether this consensus will display the domination of a present-day variety of English or the development of a new, composite variety.

Messages for the consumer

Although most of the recent educational debate has inevitably focused upon the role of SE in the United Kingdom, the future power and value of the concept will derive from its role in the international situation. It is therefore important for any course dealing with SE to inculcate awareness of what is happening to the language worldwide. Here, three points are paramount:

1. There is no longer a single kind of SE, but several, linked to the identities of the major English-speaking nations. The concept of 'regional standards' now holds centre stage.
2. In this setting, the prestige of British SE can no longer be assumed. Indeed, in several parts of the world, it has lost prestige and is an unacceptable model. This presents the British with an uncomfortable contrast to its prestige-laden role within the UK.
3. A World SE exists, but is still at a fairly primitive stage of development – in a similar position to that of British SE at the beginning of the fifteenth century (and actually with a less predictable future, for there are now several centres of gravity pulling the language in different directions.)

Children and curriculum designers need to be preparing now for the questions of consumer choice which will be presented by this multi-standard world. Indeed, it may be no more than a few decades before we find the evolution of a fresh controversy in the UK: 'Should World Standard English be taught at Key Stage 1?'

Bibliography

Achebe, C. (1964) *Arrow of God*. London: Heinemann.

Achebe, C. (1975) The African writer and the English language. In *Morning Yet on Creation Day*. London: Heinemann.

Allen, D. (1980) *English Teaching since 1965 – How much Growth?* London: Heinemann.

Alleyne, M. (1980) *Comparative Afro-American*. Ann Arbor, Mich.: Karoma.

Alleyne, M. (1989) *The Roots of Jamaican Culture*. London: Pluto Press.

Alptekin, C. and Alptekin, M. (1990) The question of culture: EFL teaching in non-English-speaking countries. In Rossner, R. and Bolitho, R. (eds) *Currents of Change in English Language Teaching*. Oxford: Oxford University Press.

Angelotti, M. (1981) Uses of young adult literature in the eighties, or life in a quiet pond ain't the same after a stone is thrown, *English in Texas*, 13: 32–4.

Asante, B. S., Pardo, W. E. and Schniedewind, N. (1991) Afro-centric curriculum, *Educational Leadership*, 49(4): 28–31.

Bain, R., Fitzgerald, B. and Taylor, M. (eds) (1992) *Looking into Language*. Sevenoaks: Hodder & Stoughton.

Bakhtin, M. (1981) *The Dialogic Imagination*. Austin, Tex: University of Texas Press.

Barnes, D. (1969) Language in the secondary classroom. In Barnes, D., Britton, J. and Rosen, H. (eds) *Language, the Learner and the School*. Harmondsworth: Penguin.

Barnes, D. and Todd, F. (1977) *Communication and Learning in Small Groups*. London: Routledge & Kegan Paul.

Ben-Hayyim, Z. (1953) *Language in a New Reality*. Jerusalem: Leshonenu La'am.

Bennett, L. (1966) *Jamaica Labrish*. Kingston: Sangsters.

Bernstein, H. (1984) *What Literature Should Adolescents be Reading?* Alexandria, Va: Association for Supervision and Curriculum Development (ED 245 228).

Bialik, C. L. (1930) Covering and uncovering language. In *Collected Essays*. Jerusalem: Dvir.

Bickerton, D. (1981) *Roots of Language*. Ann Arbor, Mich. Karoma.

Blume, J. (1974) *Blubber*. Scarsdale, NY: Bradbury Press.

Bourdieu, P. (1977) *Reproduction in Education, Society and Culture*. London: Sage.

Bourdieu, P. (1993) *The Field of Cultural Production: Essays on Art and Literature*. Cambridge: Polity Press.

Britton, J., Burgess, T., Martin, N., McLeod, A. and Rosen, H. (1975) *The Development of Writing Abilities (11–18)*. London: Macmillan Education.

Buber, M. (1955) Education. In *Between Man and Man*, trans. Smith, R. G. Boston: Beacon Press.

Cameron, D. and Bourne, J. (1989) *Grammar, Nation and Citizenship: Kingman in Linguistic and Historical Perspective*. London: Institute of Education.

Carrington, L. (1988a) *Language Without Culture – a Learner's Option*. Text of an address to a plenary session of the TESL Conference, Toronto.

Carrington, L. (1988b) Creole Discourse and Social Development. Report for the International Development Research Centre, Ottawa.

Carter, A. (1989) *Up Country*. New York: Putnam.

Carter, R. (ed.) (1990) *Knowledge About Language and the Curriculum: the LINC Reader*. Sevenoaks: Hodder & Stoughton.

Carter, R. A. and Nash, W. (1990) *Seeing Through Language: A Guide to Styles of English Writing*. Oxford: Blackwell.

Cary, L. (1991) *Black Ice*. New York: Knopf.

Chafe, W. (1986) Writing in the perspective of speaking. In Cooper, R. and Greenbaum, S. (eds) *Studying Writing*. Newbury Park, Cal.: Sage.

Cliff, M. (1988) A journey into speech. In Simonson, R. and Walker, S. (eds) *The Graywolf Annual Five: Multicultural Literacy*. St. Paul, Minn.: Graywolf Press.

Cook, G. (1992) *The Discourse of Advertising*. London: Routledge.

Cooper, C. (1989 and 1990) Slackness hiding from culture: erotic play in the dancehall (Parts 1 and 2), *Jamaica Journal*, 22(4): 12–20; 23(1): 44–51.

Cormier, R. (1977). *I am the Cheese*. New York: Pantheon Books.

Craig, D. (1967) *An Experiment in Teaching English*. London: Ginn.

Craig, D. (1976) Bidialectal education: Creole and Standard in the West Indies. *International Journal of Sociology of Language*, 8: 93–134.

Craig, D. (1980) Models for educational policy in Creole-Speaking communities. In Valdman, A. and Highfield, A. (eds) *Theoretical Orientations in Creole Studies*. New York: Academic Press.

Crowley, T. (1989) *The Politics of Discourse: The Standard Language Question and British Cultural Debates*. London: Macmillan.

Crowley, T. (ed.) (1991) *Proper English? Readings in Language, History, and Cultural Identity*. London: Routledge.

Cummins, J. and Swain, M. (1986) *Bilingualism in Education*. London: Longman.

Davis, M. (1992) Censorship update. *The (NCTE) Council Chronicle*, 2(1): 13.

DeCamp, D. (1971a) Toward a generative analysis of a post-creole speech continuum. In Hymes, D. (ed.) *Pidginization and Creolization of Languages*. Cambridge: Cambridge University Press, pp. 349–70.

DeCamp, D. (1971b) The study of pidgin and creole languages. In Hymes, D. (ed.) *Pidginization and Creolization of Languages*. Cambridge: Cambridge University Press, pp. 13–39.

Department for Education (DFE) (1993) *English for Ages 5 to 16*. London: HMSO.

Department for Education (DFE) (1993) *KS3 English Anthology*. London: HMSO.

Department for Education (DFE) (1993) *Review of National Curriculum English: recommendations of the National Curriculum Council*. York: National Curriculum Council.

Department of Education and Science (DES) (1988) *Report of the Committee of Inquiry into the Teaching of English Language* (Kingman Report). London: HMSO.

Department of Education and Science (DES) (1989) *English for ages 5 to 16* (Cox Report). London: HMSO.

Department of Education and Science (DES) (1990) *English in the National Curriculum* (No. 2). London: HMSO.

Department of Education for Northern Ireland (DENI) (1988) *Education Reform in Northern Ireland: the Way Forward*. Belfast: Department of Education.

Department of Education for Northern Ireland (DENI) (1990) *Programmes of Study and Attainment Targets – English*. Belfast: HMSO.

Devonish, H. (1986) *Languages and Liberation: Creole Language politics in the Caribbean*. London: Karia Press.

Dewey, J. (1926) Mexico's educational renaissance. In Boydston, J. A. (ed.) (1984) *The Later Works, 1925–1953*, Vol. 2, 1925–1927. Carbondale: Southern Illinois Press.

Dillard, J. L. (1972) *Black English. Its History and Usage in the United States*. New York: Random House.

Dillard, J. L. (1992) *A History of American English*. London and New York: Longman.

Ereel, E. (1977) *An Introduction to the Science of Language*. Tel-Aviv: Dekel.

Fairclough, N. (ed.) (1992) *Critical Language Awareness*. London: Longman.

Fairclough, N. (1989) *Language and Power*. London: Longman.

Fanon, F. (1968) *Black Skin, White Masks*. London: McGibbon and Kee.

Farren, S. (1976) Culture and Education in Ireland. *Compass, Journal of the Irish Association for Curriculum Development*, 3(2): 22–38.

Farren, S. and Gray, B. (1993) *Evaluating the New Program of Study for English at Secondary Level*. Coleraine: University of Ulster.

Ferguson, C. (1972) Diglossia. In Giglioli, P. (ed.) *Language and Social Context*. London: Penguin.

Fetterley, J. (1978) *The Resisting Reader: A Feminist Approach to American Fiction*. Bloomington, Ind.: Indiana University Press.

Fisher, J. (1984) *Affirming the Use of Young Adult Literature in the Classroom – A Little Psychology of Reading!* Washington, D.C.: National Institute of Education (ED 245 211).

Friel, B. (1981) *Translations*. London: Faber.

Gabler, M. and Gabler, N. (1982) Mind control through textbooks. *Phi Delta Kappan*, 64(2): 96.

Gadamer, A. (1966) *Man and Language*. New York.

Gardner, J. (1972) *Grendel*. London: André Deutsch.

Görlach, M. (1988) English as a world language – the state of the art. *English World-Wide*, 9(1): 1–32.

Government of India (1948) *Report of the Education Commission*. New Delhi: Government of India Press.

Government of India (1955) *Report of the Kunzru Committee*. New Delhi: Government of India Press.

Government of India (1966) *Report of the Education Commission (1964–66)*. New Delhi: Government of India Press.

Government of India (1985) *Challenge of Education*. New Delhi: Ministry of Education.

Government of India (1986a) *National Policy on Education*. New Delhi: Ministry of Human Resource Development.

Government of India (1986b) *Programme of Action*. New Delhi: Ministry of Human Resource Development.

Grant, C. and Sleeter, C. (1988) Race, class, and gender and abandoned dreams. *Teachers College Record*, 90(1): 19–40.

Gray, S. (1979) *South Africa Literature. An Introduction.* Cape Town: David Philip.

Greene, S. (1979) *The Boy Who Drank too Much.* New York: Viking.

Hakuta, K. (1986) *Mirror of Language: the Debate on Bilingualism.* New York: Basic Books.

Hall, L. (1990) *Halsey's Pride.* New York: Scribner.

Halliday, M. A. K. (1989) *Spoken and Written Language.* Oxford: Oxford University Press.

Hamers, J. F. and Blanc, M. H. A. (1989) *Bilinguality and Bilingualism.* Cambridge: Cambridge University Press.

Hammond, J. (1990) Is learning to read the same as learning to speak? In Christie, F. (ed.) *Literacy for a Changing World.* Sydney: ACER, pp. 26–53.

Harris, R. (1980) *The Language Makers.* New York: Cornell University Press.

Harrison, B. T. (1990) Realising through writing, *Aspects of Education*, 42: 36–57.

Harrison, B. T. (1992) Encouraging positive attitudes to language and learning among multilingual/bilingual speakers in schools: principles and practice. In Hayhoe, M. and Parker, S. (eds) *Reassessing Language and Literacy.* Milton Keynes: Open University Press, pp. 36–49.

Harrison, B. T. and Mercer, E. (1992) Friels' *Translations* – applying insights for a literary text to therapeutic language teaching. *Educational Therapy and Therapeutic Teaching*, 1(1): 9–231.

Hawkes, T. (1992) *Meaning by Shakespeare.* London: Routledge.

Heaney, S. (1972) *Wintering Out.* London: Faber and Faber.

Herber, H. and Nelson-Herber, J. (1984) Planning the reading program. In Purves, A. and Niles, O. (eds) *Becoming Readers in a Complex Society.* Chicago, Ill.: University of Chicago Press.

Herbert, C. (1974) *I See A Child.* Garden City, NY: Anchor Books.

Hinton, S. E. (1967) *The Outsiders.* New York: Viking.

Hirsch, E. (1987) *Cultural Literacy: What Every American Needs to Know.* Boston: Houghton Mifflin.

Hobbs, W. (1989) *Bearstone.* New York: Atheneum.

Hodge, M. (1981) *Crick Crack Monkey.* London: Heinemann.

Hudson, R. A. (1980) *Sociolinguistics.* Cambridge: Cambridge University Press.

Jenkins, D. *et al.* (1980) *Chocolate, Cream, Soldiers: a Final Evaluation Report on 'The Schools Cultural Studies Project'.* Coleraine: New University of Ulster.

Jernudd, B. T. (1981) 'Planning language treatment: linguistics for the Third World', *Language and Society*, 10(1): 43–72.

Johnson, J. (1992) *Pamela Jean.* Bloomington, Ill.: The Write Partnership Press.

Kachru, B. B. (1992) World Englishes: approaches, issues and resources. In Kinsela, V. (ed.) *Language Teaching.* Cambridge: Cambridge University Press.

Kohl, H. (1992) I won't learn from you! Thoughts on the role of assent in learning, *Rethinking Schools*, 7(1): 1.

Kott, J. (1965) *Shakespeare our Contemporary.* London: University Paperbacks.

Kovacs, K. (1987) The quest for change in Mexican education, *Current History*, 86(518): 117–20.

Kozol, J. (1985) *Illiterate America.* New York: New American Library.

Kurath, H. (1972) *Studies in Area Linguistics.* Bloomington and London: University of Indiana Press.

Labov, W. (1972) *Sociolinguistic Patterns.* Philadelphia, Penn.: University of Pennsylvania Press.

Lee, G. (1991) *China Boy: A Novel.* New York: Dutton.

Leibowitz, A. H. (1978) *The Bilingual Education Act: A Legislative Analysis.* Rosslyn, Va.: InterAmerica Research Associates, Inc.

Leonard, M. (1988) *The 1988 Education Act: A Tactical Guide for Schools.* Oxford: Basil Blackwell.

LINC (1992) *Language in the National Curriculum (LINC): Materials for Professional Development.* Nottingham: University of Nottingham, Department of English Studies.

Lisman, D. (1989) Yes, Holden should read these books. *English Journal*, 78(4): 14–18.

Longley, E. (1993) Challenging complacency. *Fortnight*, March, 20–24.

Lozano, L. (1991) *Español Activo, Tercer Curso*, 17th edn, Mexico, D.F.: Libris Editores.

Lyons, F. L. S. (1979) *Culture and Anarchy in Ireland 1890–1939.* Oxford: Clarendon Press.

Lyons, J. (1981) *Language and Linguistics.* Cambridge: Cambridge University Press.

Malone, J. and Crone, R. (1975) A new approach to innovation in schools. *The Northern Teacher*, 12(1): 16–20.

Marbach, A. (1991) A Comparative Study of the Teaching of the Mother Tongue in Britain and in Israel (Unpublished PhD thesis). Sheffield: University of Sheffield.

Marckwardt, A. H. (1980) *American English.* Revised by Dillard, J. L. Oxford: Oxford University Press.

McCarthy, M. and Carter, R. (1993) *Language as Discourse: Perspectives for Language Teaching.* Longman: Harlow.

McCrum, R., Cran, W. and MacNeil, R. (1986) *The Story of English.* New York: Viking.

McGinley, W. and Kamberelis, W. (1992) Transformative functions of children's writing. *Language Arts*, 69(5): 330–7.

Menchu, R. (1984) *I Rigoberta Menchu, A Guatemalan Indian Woman.* London: Verso.

Merleau-Ponty, M. (1974) *Phenomenology, Language and Society.* London: Heinemann.

Milroy, J. and Milroy, L. (1991) *Authority in Language*, 2nd edn. London: Routledge.

National Association of Teachers of English (Jamaica) (1992) *Journal of English Teachers.* Kingston: NATE.

Ngugi, J. (1965) *The River Between.* London: Heinemann.

Nichols, G. (1990) The battle with language. In Cudjoe, S. R. (ed.) *Caribbean Women Writers. Essays from the First International Conference.* Wellesley: Calaloux Publications.

Nida, E. (1975) *Language Study and Translation.* Stanford: Stanford University Press.

Northern Ireland Curriculum Council (NICC) (1989a) *Cross-Curricular Themes: Consultation Report.* Belfast: NICC.

Northern Ireland Curriculum Council (NICC) (1989b) *Cultural Heritage: A Cross-Curricular Theme, Report of the Cross Curricular Working Group on Cultural Heritage.* Belfast: NICC.

Nugent, S. (1984) Adolescent literature: a transition into a future of reading. *English Journal*, 73(7): 35–37.

O'Donnell, H. (1984) Where does adolescent literature belong?. *English Journal*, 73(7): 84–86.

Omodiaogbe, S. (1992) 150 years on: English in the Nigerian school system – past, present and future, *English Language Teaching Journal*, 46(1): 19–28.

Ong, W. (1982) On saying We and Us to literature'. In Baker, H. (ed.) *Three American Literatures: Essays in Chicano, Native American, and Asian-American Literature for*

Teachers of American Literature. New York: Modern Language Association of America.

Orlev, U. (1991) *The Man from the Other Side*. Boston: Houghton Mifflin.

Ormsby, F. (ed.) (1991) *The Collected Poems of John Hewitt*. Belfast: The Blackstaff Press.

Otto, W. (1992) Readers R us, *Journal of Reading*, 36(4): 318–320.

Parrinder, P. (1993) Nationalising English, *London Review of Books*, 28 January.

Paterson, K. (1977) *Bridge to Terabithia*. New York: Crowell.

Paterson, K. (1991) *Lyddie*. New York: Lodestar Press.

Peled, E. (1975) *Education in the Eighties*. Jerusalem: Ministry of Education.

Perera, K. (1990) Grammatical differentiation between speech and writing in children aged 8–12. In Carter, R. (ed.) *Knowledge about Language and the Curriculum*. Sevenoaks: Hodder and Stoughton.

Pollard, V. (1983a) The social history of Dread Talk. In Carrington, L. (ed.) with Craig, D. and Dandaré, R. *Studies in Caribbean Language*. St Augustine, Trinidad: Society for Caribbean Linguistics, pp. 46–62.

Pollard, V. (1983b) The classroom teacher and the standard language, *Caribbean Journal of Education*, 10(1): 33–44.

Pollard, V. (1992) The Lexicon of Dread Talk in Standard Jamaican English. Paper presented to the Ninth Biennial Conference of the Society for Caribbean Linguistics, Cave Hill, Barbados.

Probst, R. (1987) Adolescent literature and the English curriculum. *English Journal*, 76(3): 26–30.

Quirk, R., Greenbaum, S., Leech, G. and Svartvik, J. (1985) *A Comprehensive Grammar of the English Language*. London: Longman.

Rao, R. (1938) *Kanthapura*. London: Allen and Unwin.

Robinson, A. (1981) *The Schools Cultural Studies Project – Director's Report*. Coleraine: New University of Ulster.

Rogers, J. (1990) The world for sick proper. In Rossner, R. and Bolitho, R. (eds) *Currents of Change in the English Language*. Oxford: Oxford University Press 7–15.

Rohlehr, G. (1989) The Shape of that Hurt. In Brown, S., Morris, M. and Rohlehr, G. (eds) *Voiceprint: an Anthology of Oral and Related Poetry for the Caribbean*. Harlow: Longman.

Romaine, S. (1989) *Bilingualism*. Oxford: Blackwell.

Rosenblatt, L. (1982) The literary transaction: evocation and response. *Theory into Practice*, 21(4): 268–77.

Scholes, R. (1985) *Textual Power: Literary Theory and the Teaching of English*. New Haven, Conn.: Yale University Press.

Schools Examinations and Assessment Council (SEAC) (1993a) *Key Stage Three School Assessment Folder/1993 Audit of Teacher Assessment*. London: Ref A/055/B/92.

Schools Examinations and Assessment Council (SEAC) (1993b) *Key Stage Three School Assessment Folder/Information on the 1993 Tests/English*. London: Ref A/059/B/92.

Secretaría de Educacíon Publica (SEP) (1991a) *Programa para la modernización educativa, Propuesta de programa nacional de Lengua y Literature, Secundaria 1er grado*. Mexico: D.F.

Secretaría de Educacíon Publica (SEP) (1991b) *Programa para la modernización educativa, Propuesta de programa nacional de Lengua y Literature, Secundaria 2o grado*. Mexico, D.F.: SEP.

Secretaría de Educacíon Publica (SEP) (1992) *Acuerdo Nacional para la Modernización de la Educación Básica.* Mexico, D.F.: SEP.

Shields, K. (1989) Standard English in Jamaica: a case of competing models. *English World-Wide*, 10(1): 41–53.

Shields, K. (1992) The folk come of age: variation and change in language use on air in Jamaica. Paper presented to the Association for Commonwealth Literature and Language Studies, Mona, Jamaica.

Skilbeck, M. (1976) Education and cultural change. *Compass: Journal of the Irish Association for Curriculum Development*, 5(2): 3–23.

Smilansky, Y. (1972) *Stop Teaching Literature.* Jerusalem: Hachinuch.

Stenhouse, L. (1975) *An Introduction to Curriculum Research and Development.* London: Heinemann.

Stubbs, M. (1976) Keeping in touch. In Stubbs, M. and Delamont, S. (eds) *Explorations in Classroom Observations.* London: Wiley.

Stubbs, M. (1980) *Language and Literacy: the Sociolinguistics of Reading and Writing.* London: Routledge.

Stubbs, M. (1983) *Language, Schools and Classrooms*, 2nd edn. London: Methuen.

Stubbs, M. (1987) An educational theory of (written) language. In *Written Language* (British Studies in Applied Linguistics). London: CILT.

Tadmor, J. (1989) *Revolution or Development in Education.* Tel Aviv: Davar.

Tannen, D. (1982) Oral and literature strategies in spoken and written narratives, *Language*, 58(1): 1–21.

Tannen, D. (1989) *Talking Voices: Repetition, Dialogue and Imagery in Conversational Discourse.* Cambridge: Cambridge University Press.

Thomas, G. (1991) *Linguistic Purism.* London: Longman.

Trudgill, P. and Hannah, J. (1982) *International English. A Guide to Varieties of Standard English.* London: Edward Arnold.

Ullman, S. (1962) *Semantics.* Oxford: Oxford University Press.

University Grants Commission (1978) *Report of the Working Group.* New Delhi: UGC Press.

Van der Staay, S. (1992) Doing theory: words about words about *The Outsiders. English Journal*, 81(7): 57–61.

Walder, D. (1992) 'Studying post-colonial literature'. In Walder, D. (ed.) *Post-colonial Literature in English (A421 Study Guide).* Milton Keynes: The Open University.

Wilkinson, A. (1975) *Language and Education.* Oxford: Oxford University Press.

Wilkinson, A. (1982) The implication of Oracy. In Wade, B. (ed.) *Language Perspectives.* London: Heinemann.

Williams, R. (1977) *Marxism and Literature.* Oxford: Oxford University Press.

Williams, R. (1983) *Keywords*, 2nd edn. London: Fontana.

Williamson, L. (1978) To climb their success ladder. In Marcus, D. (ed.) *Pockets of Hope, an Anthology of Poetry on Teaching and Learning.* Unpublished.

Yeats, W. B. (1961) *Collected Poems.* London: Macmillan.

Index

community, culture and, 79–80
conservative pluralism, 9
consumer choice, 108, 114
continuum theory, 44, 100
Cook, G., 16
Cooper, C., 105
Cormier, Robert, *I Am the Cheese*, 86
count nouns, 22
Cox Report, 28, 51
Craig, D., 104, 105–6
creativity
    English as medium of, 63–4
    translation and, 47–9
Creole, 44, 99, 100, 101–2, 103–7
Cristero War, 54
Crone, R., 26
cross-curricular themes, 27–8
Crowley, T., 22, 73, 75
cultural analysis, 29, 31
cultural capital, 37–8, 39–40
cultural fields, 37–8
cultural heritage, 25, 26, 27–32
    cross-curricular approach, 27–8
    and English, 28–31
    likelihood of success, 31–2
cultural transmission, 98–9, 101, 107
    see also Jamaica
culture, 84
    acculturation, 86–7
    and community in language, 79–80
    defining, 27–8
    English's absorption of foreign, 63
Cummins, J., 44

dancehall music, 104–5
Davis, M., 86
DeCamp, D., 100, 101
Department for Education (DFE), 15
Department of Education for Northern Ireland
    (DENI)
    Education Reform in Northern Ireland,
        27
    Programmes of Study for English, 25
Department of Education and Science (DES)
    Cox Report, 28, 51
    Kingman Report, 50, 98
Devlin, Polly, 29
Devonish, H., 44–5, 100, 102
Dewey, John, 54
dialect, 79
    American English, 74
    bidialectalism, 81, 105
    Caribbean, 43–4, 99–100, 101–7
dialogue, 52
diglossia, 99–100
Dillard, J. L., 70, 73, 74–5
diphthongs, centralized, 74
discussion, class, 51–2, 95
distinctiveness, 113–14
Dixon, John, 91–2
dramatic effect, 35
Dread Talk, 102–3
dub poetry, 104
'dummy runs', 92

education for mutual understanding, 26, 27
Education Reform Act (1988), 49, 86
educational reforms
    Mexico and England compared, 53–4, 58–61
    testing and league tables, 33–4, 41
educational research, 60
educational system, 81
elitist education, 64–5
empowerment, 75–6
English as a Foreign Language (EFL), 98
English as a Native Language (ENL), 98
English as a Second Language (ESL), 98
Ereel, E., 46

Fanon, Franz, 43, 98
Farren, S., 25, 29, 31
Ferguson, C., 99
Fetterley, J., 87
financial accountability, 1–2
Fisher, Jan, 88
freedom, teachers', 49
French, 63, 80–1
Friel, Brian, *Translations*, 48
full-time education, parents' legal obligations
    and, 2–3

Gabler, M., 89
Gabler, N., 89
Gadamer, A., 48–9
Gardner, John, *Grendel*, 86
German, 63
global link language, 45, 62, 98–9, 100–1,
    113–14
Government of India
    Challenge of Education, 66
    Education Commissions, 65
    Kunzru Committee, 65
    National Policy on Education, 66
    Programmes of Action, 66
government regulation of curriculum,
    see National Curriculum
grammar, spoken and written, 11–23
Grant, C., 86
Gray, B., 29, 31
Greene, Shep, *The Boy Who Drank Too
    Much*, 86
Griffiths, Brian, 98
Guatemala, 79–80

habitus, 38
Hakuta, K., 44
Hall, Lynn, *Halsey's Pride*, 87
Halliday, Michael, *Spoken and Written
    Language*, 16–17
Hamers, J. F., 44
Hammond, J., 20
Hannah, J., 70
    International English, 71–2
Harbinson, John, 29
Harris, R., 68
Harrison, B. T., 44, 48
Hawkes, Terence, *Meaning by Shakespeare*, 38
Heaney, Seamus, 29
    'The Other Side', 29–31

ENGLISH PEOPLE
THE EXPERIENCE OF TEACHING AND LEARNING ENGLISH IN BRITISH UNIVERSITIES

Colin Evans

English People is a portrait of the subject 'English' as it is experienced by teachers and students in British Higher Education. The author has interviewed staff and students in the Universities of Cardiff, Newcastle, Oxford and Stirling and in the former Polytechnic of North London (now the University of North London). These 'English People' speak of the impact of Theory, of Feminism, of the experience of reading and writing, of the problems of teaching literature, of the peculiarities of Oxford and of compulsory Anglo-Saxon, of post-colonial literature and of academic leadership in a time of financial pressure.

English People is also an example of the way in which nations attempt to produce unity out of ethnic diversity by using the national education system and especially the subject which has the name of the national language. It questions whether 'English' can still produce unity and whether it has unity itself. Is 'English', like the British Isles, a varied archipelago and not a land mass? Has it deconstructed itself out of existence?

The book is about students and teachers who have made this choice of subject and career, and is fascinating reading for past, present and aspiring students and teachers of English, in universities, colleges and schools. It is also relevant to anyone interested in Higher Education and its organization.

Contents
Part 1: Joining – Origins – Choice – Reading and writing – Teaching and learning – Life in an institution – Part 2: Dividing – Male/female – Theory – Discipline – English, Englishes and the English – Postface – Appendix – Notes – Bibliography – Index.

256pp   0 335 09359 0 (Paperback)   0 335 09361 2 (Hardback)

WORDSWORTH NOW AND THEN
ROMANTICISM AND CONTEMPORARY CULTURE

Antony Easthope

Conventional criticism discusses Wordsworth's poetry in terms of what his writing might have meant *then*, around 1800. Antony Easthope writes about how we can read that poetry *now*, nearly 200 years on. His Wordsworth is produced by the ideologies of Romanticism but is also our contemporary, a poet to be read alongside today's popular culture (if Wordsworth has regrets about his past, so does Frank Sinatra). In a lucid and accessible manner Professor Easthope draws on recent critical theory to show how Wordsworth's poetry works, how the love of Nature, sincere personal experience and telling the truth about yourself all come about as effects of language.

At once irreverent and scholarly, politically engaged and drily witty, Easthope's analysis imports an intellectual seriousness to the discussion of Wordsworth that is missing in his sentimental admirers. In bringing these texts from then to life now, this compact and daring book is a model for how to re-read canonical works. Its implications for the practice of literary criticism are far-reaching – and Wordsworth will never be the same again.

Contents
Nature and imagination – Romantic ideology – The Wordsworth experience – Autobiography 1: theme – Autobiography 2: rhetoric – Gender – Language – The heart of a heartless world – Notes – Index.

176pp   0 335 09460 0 (Paperback)   0 335 09461 9 (Hardback)

THE TEXTS OF PAULO FREIRE

Paul V. Taylor

Paulo Freire can be numbered among the few great educators this century. His classroom is the world of the oppressed: his subject is the literacy of liberation.

This volume provides a (re)introduction to Freire. The first part is a fresh, biographical sketch of his life, the context within which he worked and the texts which he has produced. The second part uncovers the genius of his eclecticism and discovers that, contrary to the myth, his revolutionary method is more a radical reinvention of classical pedagogy.

This sets the scene for a review and questioning of Freire's method and of his philosophy of contradiction. There is then critical examination of his view of literacy through a close reading of the teaching material on which his successful method is based.

The concluding section attempts to reconstruct a practice of literacy, illustrating the importance of Freire's pedagogy of questioning for all those who are working in the field of literacy today.

Contents

Introduction: The textualizing and contextualizing of Freire – A biographical sketch – Backgrounds and borrowings: a review of selected sources and influences – Education and liberation: the means and ends of Dialogue and Conscientization – The 'Método Paulo Freire': generative words and generating literacy – Generating literacy: decoding Freire's ten learning situations – A reconstruction of literacy – Conclusion – Notes – Bibliographies – Index.

176pp   0 335 19019 7 (Paperback)   0 335 19020 0 (Hardback)